From Where I Stood

The Delivery of a Medical School

Sabine Alston Goodman Andrews

From Where I Stood

*The Delivery
of a
Medical School*

✚

Sabine Alston
Goodman Andrews
PARTNER EMERITA

Copyright © 2009 Sabine Alston Goodman Andrews

All rights reserved. No part of this publication may be reproduced, stored in a retrieval system, or transmitted, in any form or by any means, electronic, mechanical, photocopying, recording, or otherwise, without the written prior permission of the author.

Published by arrangement with Parke Press, Norfolk, Virginia.

Parke Press is committed to making it possible for writers to tell their stories and affordably deliver them to readers interested in intimate social histories which, collectively, tell the story of our region and our world.
Parke Press will continue the tradition of fine book making and employ graphic aesthetics that encourage reading and readability.

To find out how to publish your book and make it available worldwide, please contact us at parkepress@cox.net

10 9 8 7 6 5 4 3 2 1

Printed in the United States of America.
ISBN 978-0-9843339-0-5 *(Soft)*

Library of Congress Cataloging-in-Publication Data
Available upon request

AUTHOR'S NOTE

ESTABLISHING THE Eastern Virginia Medical School was a creative act by citizens of Norfolk and Hampton Roads who wanted excellent medical care for the residents of their area.

That they were able to overcome formidable obstacles was a result of a successful leadership methodology, the description of which others may find useful.

The person most qualified to tell the story, my husband Mason Andrews, resisted repeated entreaties to write of this or of his subsequent activities with EVMS and with the City of Norfolk. Mason was too busy moving forward to address past accomplishments. Hence, these pages attempt to tell some of the highlights of the story by some who lived closely with the story.

July 2009

ACKNOWLEDGMENTS

SINCERE APPRECIATION IS EXPRESSED to the following persons for their encouragement and/or editorial assistance: Mason M. Andrews, M.Arch., editor-in-chief; Jean A. Andrews, M.A.; Roseann Runte, C.M., Ph.D., D.Litt., FRSC; Howard W. Jones, Jr., M.D.; Richardson K. Noback, M.D.; Robert J. Faulconer, M.D.; Nancy Garcia; Marshall McClure; and to Margery L. Krome, M.U.A.

TABLE OF CONTENTS

Author's Note v
Acknowledgments vi
Prelude ix

1 Norfolk in 1950 – First Impressions 1
2 Clearing the Way 4
3 Learning What a Team Can Accomplish 8
4 Opening Salvos 14
5 Making the Case for a Medical School 17
6 In Search of a Designated Driver 21
7 City and State Help in Early Organization 23
8 Expert Advice Nets a Hunting License 26
9 The NAMCA Team Goes to Work 30
10 Portrait of a Leader 32
11 The Medical Center Motel 35
12 Dr. Andrews Goes to Washington 39
13 In Search of an Academic Affiliation 42
14 Growing Pains – Securing a Site 47
15 Picking Up the Tab 54
16 Launch! 59
17 The Heart Starts Beating 63
18 To School for the School 66
19 Continuing to Lead 69

Afterword 72

Appendices 73
Appendix 1: Resolution by Norfolk Area Medical Center
Authority 73
Appendix 2: Letter from Richardson K. Noback, M.D., of
April 19, 1970 74
Appendix 3: Letter from Robert T. Manning, M.D., of
May 20, 1971 76
Appendix 4: Letter from Vernon E. Wilson, M.D.,
of March 2, 1973 78
Appendix 5: Letter from Vernon E. Wilson, M.D.,
of June 15, 1973 80
Appendix 6: Letter from Robert T. Manning, M.D., of
December 6, 1976 81
Appendix 7: Commentary by Richardson K. Noback, M.D.,
of July, 2008 82
Appendix 8: Editorial perspective, Richardson K. Noback,
of September 17, 2008 84
Appendix 9: Mason C. Andrews' 1983 Draft Timeline 87
Appendix 10: EVMS Announcement concerning
Andrews Hall, 2007 90

PRELUDE

WHILE VISITING MY COLLEGE ROOMMATE and her family at Virginia Beach in 1943, I met Mason Andrews. He was then a fourth-year medical student at Johns Hopkins, soon to receive his M.D. degree and be inducted into the U.S. Navy as a Lieutenant (j.g.) in World War II service. I was totally astonished by the conversational contention that ensued with this friend of my friend. We each survived the encounter, but surely with no inkling that we would later embark on an adventure together of nearly sixty years.

Five years later, as an ear surgery patient at Johns Hopkins Hospital, I found myself on the receiving end of a curious courtship of sorts. I was reintroduced to Mason by my college friend. He was then chief resident on the obstetrical service there. He lost little time demonstrating his gift for delegation by dispatching another to take his place for the first date (a movie being shown in another part of the hospital). To be fair, he had been called to help manage a difficult case. To make amends the next morning, he brought boxes of index cards to my hospital room and enlisted my help in sorting information they contained for a scientific paper in progress on Fallopian tubes. Forewarned, then, I was — although the extent to which my future would reflect the courtship I could not possibly have imagined.

When Mason returned to Norfolk in 1950 to join his father's practice of obstetrics and gynecology, he brought with him educational assets gleaned at Princeton, at the Johns Hopkins Medical School, and in the U.S. Navy, together with two sea bags of unwashed socks and me, his bride of three months.

Mason and Sabine Andrews on September 24, 1949

I

Norfolk in 1950 – First Impressions

As a newcomer and Mason's wife, I heard Norfolk characterized as "this old seaport city" which had survived fire, siege, and epidemic. The reputation acquired during World War I for inhospitality to military personnel was still being mentioned. The sedate and conservative pace and style of life — and wardrobe preferences — reflected its English influence, I was told, while a huge stock of slum housing blighted both lives and landscape.

I was to learn that, under this discouraging exterior, there existed a will and a spirit to achieve and improve that was remarkable and was to carry this area far. Perhaps it was born of survival philosophy, but I was told that in 1934, Norfolk's will and spirit had begun to stir into action. In that year, a citizens' commission began to examine the causes of crime in the city of Norfolk. It concluded that the huge amount of significantly substandard housing loomed large among the causes, and recommended correction to the city government. This led to the establishment of the Norfolk Housing Authority in the 1940's.

The citizens' commission included Mr. Charles Kaufman, a Norfolk attorney and community benefactor. Those who were privileged to know this incredibly able and dedicated man were filled with admiration for his accomplishments and delighted to find themselves in his company. He had a twinkle in his eye and was the modest, unassuming gentle person one finds great men to be. He was "Mr. Norfolk" in many hearts and minds.

At about the time the Housing Authority was established, another group of local citizen leaders that included Mr. Kaufman met to consider the problems of the United Community Fund, the umbrella group under which many non-profit health and human services were funded locally. Intent that the Fund would henceforth meet its annual goals, it developed a strategy of involving successful local business talent and, most importantly perhaps, of mobilizing and training citizen leadership. This strategy enhanced the ability of these leaders to plan and work together, a practice that has been vital to so much progress in this area. I was told that if anything could be credited with giving Norfolk its "can-do" attitude, it would be this concerted effort. That the local United Fund (now United Way) drives have achieved or exceeded their goals very consistently since that time, something of a record nationally, speaks to the enduring will and spirit to achieve that Norfolk's people have so frequently lent to civic endeavor.

Alumni of United Fund efforts turned their ability to work together and achieve in 1946, a time at which the quality of city government was judged to be inadequate by many thoughtful citizens. On a promise to serve but one term as a good government demonstration, the "citizen ticket" of Cooke-Darden-Twohy was elected to Norfolk City Council. These councilmen served for only one term, as promised during their campaign, but they were able to imbue the city government with a strong focus on executive talent and responsiveness to human need.

The Norfolk City Council of this era worked closely with what was by then the Norfolk Redevelopment and Housing Authority. Because of its previous groundwork, the Authority was in a position to undertake the first federally funded slum clearance project in the United States in 1951.

I was by then in a position to observe events first hand against the foregoing history. An indelible image in my mind is that of Mr. Kaufman, in his capacity as chairman of the board of Norfolk Redevelopment and Housing Authority, literally in the driver's seat of the first bulldozer to take aim at some of Norfolk's worst slum housing.

Mr. Charles Kaufman and NRHA Director Larry Cox inaugurate the first slum clearance project in the United States

2

CLEARING THE WAY

ASTRIDE THE BULLDOZER with Mr. Kaufman on that day in 1951 when Norfolk's slums began to fall was Lawrence M. Cox, Executive Director of the Norfolk Redevelopment and Housing Authority (NRHA). Larry, who later achieved national prominence as HUD Secretary George W. Romney's first assistant secretary in the Nixon Administration, and as president of the American Association of Planning Officials, led NRHA through its most far-reaching and creative period.

In the 1950's, the extent of NRHA's activity was massive: it had cleared more land than any other U.S. city. By mid-century, slum conditions had tended to develop in many old, crowded, eastern cities. Locally, the slumlord tended to be a "respectable citizen" and municipal eyes looked the other way.

Today, in Norfolk's thriving center city, it is impossible for anyone who did not see Norfolk's slums in the 1950's to conceive of what existed there. Even for those who were here it may be difficult to remember just how horrific it was.

The cancer eating at the core of Norfolk included acres of dilapidated, rat-infested, firetrap buildings without indoor plumbing. Outdoor privies on dirt lanes were surrounded by tons of uncollected trash and garbage. The desperate humanity housed there was being preyed upon by

Central Norfolk prior to NRHA-led slum clearances

landowners exploiting human misery for profit. Pervasive hopelessness often erupted into street crime, or worse.

NRHA's staff was excellent, its board of commissioners competent and dedicated. Together they combined vision and persistence with sensitivity and restraint where possible as its activity widened.

The accomplishments of NRHA instilled an awakening sense of possibility and hope for the future in Norfolk. The strategy in Norfolk was radical — to re-imagine and remake the center city. It would be difficult to overstate the NRHA's beneficial influence on what Norfolk in the 1950's became or exaggerate the possibilities it opened for what Norfolk might become.

ONE AREA OF REDEVELOPMENT activity in which much sub-standard housing had been cleared was a section of Norfolk known as Atlantic City. Atlantic City was also the site of the old Norfolk General Hospital, long overdue for expansion.

Visionary leaders frequently are found working on more than one good cause at a time. Mr. Kaufman was the president of the hospital board of directors on which the talented and creative Larry Cox also sat. When a brochure was needed describing the proposal to replace the old West Wing of Norfolk General Hospital with a new building, for fund drive purposes, Mr. Kaufman delegated the task to Larry.

At that time the King's Daughters, dedicated to children's health care, were operating an outpatient and visiting nurse service and a "hospital" of sorts in an old building on Yarmouth Street. Doctors' offices were widely scattered, as were the city's public health facilities.

Larry Cox wore two hats. At NRHA the consolidation of these disparately located medical facilities seemed an appealing reuse of some of the newly cleared land in the Atlantic City area which had room for more than a new hospital building. Plans progressed at NRHA to include a children's hospital, a city health department building, and a doctors' office building. But as Larry pondered the scope of the plan with NRHA, he raised further questions: What facilities should be contained in a modern medical center for a region in which one-fourth of the state's population resided? He became concerned that the present plan was too limited. Should it contain a school of medicine?

Larry broached the idea with colleagues, and in an address to the Ryan Club. The press reported the idea was favorably received there. It was later, in 1961, at the well-attended dedication of a new doctors' office building near the hospital — the Medical Tower — that the case for a medical school was first presented to a wider public.

3

LEARNING WHAT A TEAM CAN ACCOMPLISH

IT WAS WITH THE DEVELOPMENT, design and construction of the Medical Tower that our family began its intimate involvement with the unfolding of this tale. During the intervening decade following his return to Norfolk, Mason had taken his turn as president of the Norfolk General Hospital staff and was, at that time, president-elect of the Norfolk County Medical Society, following Dr. John Franklin.

The presidency of the Medical Tower Development Corporation, however, was a challenge of a very different sort. There was no MBA degree in Mason's black doctor's bag. He did, however, hold several convictions, which more than a few of us heard repeatedly over the course of decades of projects: "If you're persuaded something is worth doing, then you set about trying to do it well." "Assemble the most knowledgeable people and the best advice you can." This was clearly a job for experts, and, to achieve the desired superior result, the experts had to be superior indeed.

The real estate developer associated with the project was S. L. Nusbaum Company, with V. H. "Pooch" Nusbaum acting as the project's principal agent. Pooch successfully promoted the project to prospective tenants, and at dedication the building received its 81 charter doctors,

Norfolk General Staff, 9 October 1961. Left side, back row: [unidentified], Bill Sellers, [unidentified], Howard Kruger, W. Arthur Porter, Levi Old, [unidentified], [unidentified], Bob McAlpine, Pat Devine, Bob Payne, Jr., Newt Van Horn, [unidentified], Themis Pangolos, [unidentified]. Front row: Claiborne Fitchett. Right side, back row: [unidentified], Julius Snyder, Bill Hotchkiss, Sam McDaniel, Clancy Trower, Mallory Andrews, [unidentified], [unidentified], Arnold Zetlin, Ira Cantin, Bill Hoover, Bryan Grinnan. Front row: Charles Devine, Jr., Bill Old

surgeons, dentists, and also supporting technical personnel, totaling 94 tenants. Although it was common knowledge that 80 doctors might be unable to agree even on what day it was, everyone seemed jubilant. Initial tenants contributed funds sufficient to secure construction and mortgage funding. Mason's particular compensation, beyond the successful completion of a project with a talented team, was a pewter llama tie clip from Pooch, worn daily and with affection for as long as he lived.

Vincent G. Kling of Philadelphia, also architect for Norfolk's city hall complex, was chosen as principal architect, in association with the

Vincent Kling and Associates in the 1960s

local firm of Oliver and Smith. Vincent Kling's wealth of experience included the successful design of medical facilities, such as Lankanau Hospital in Philadelphia. His meticulous personal attention to the project included the redesign of the building, to accommodate roughly one-third of medical practitioners in Norfolk, from rectangular to square to achieve enhanced function and economy, and a determination to create an exterior finish designed "to reflect the beautiful Tidewater sunsets."

Vincent also advocated the association of Gilbane Building Company, of Providence, R.I., which had a compelling reputation for large-scale construction, and so brought William J. Gilbane, executive vice-president, to the conference table. The finished building more than fulfilled hopes and expectations, and it is fully functional more than forty-seven years later.

On the home front, large cartons of documents from the project began arriving with the obvious intention of becoming part of the décor.

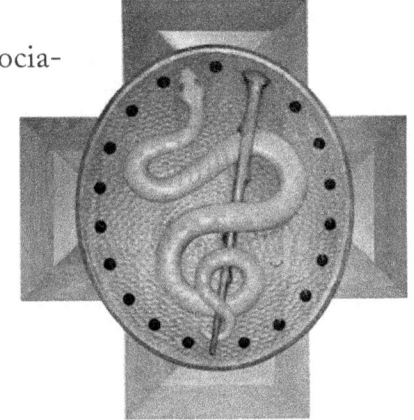

The Medical Tower's Symbol, the Caduceus of Asclepius, carved by a professor of sculpture at the University of Pennsylvania

Regular construction supervision by the president of the Medical Tower Development Corporation involved hoisting wife and children on a board-and-rope lift outside the building, to see the view from the top. All participated in the months-long search by jeep and on foot for the perfect live oak tree for the courtyard of the Medical Tower. The tree was transplanted to an island in a reflecting pool, now filled. Mason was so taken with this element of Vincent's design that he defended its preservation even after an unfortunate patient was blown into it on a windy day and it became known, perhaps not wholly admiringly, as "Mason's Basin."

Medical Tower Courtyard

As it happened, the original tree did not survive more than a few years after transplanting. A search was mounted again by jeep in the vast acreage of an outlying nursery. The replacement choice was found to have a faded tag wired to it that read "Andrews. Choice 2." Although the pool has long since been filled in, the tree still thrives at the Medical Tower.

That the project had been great fun must be credited to the people involved who knew how to make it work well. The newspaper had run an editorial in December, just prior to the Medical Tower's opening, entitled "A New Star Over Norfolk". This was generated in part as a response to a light display consisting of selectively illuminated windows in the building outlining a Christmas tree finished with a three-dimensional star atop the building. It was another of Mason's project embellishments for which he enlisted the talents of local artist Alice Armistead. It was hard to miss how much Mason enjoyed the project, and how firmly to heart he took the large lesson it demonstrated to him about the rewards to be realized by working with a group of people of good will and talent.

If the Medical Tower represents a lesson in how a dream could be realized for the public good, a particularly poignant endorsement was unearthed during the preparation for the move to his new office there: Mason discovered a personal letter from Mr. David Pender, representing most probably the board of the Norfolk General Hospital. The letter was addressed to Mason's father, Dr. C. J. Andrews, and stated the need to plan for a doctors' office building near Norfolk General Hospital "when the war is over" (WW II).

Indeed, in 1957 Dr. George A. Duncan, an orthopedist, urged by his partner, Dr. John A. Thiemeyer, Jr., had led a group to develop the idea for such a building. Dr. C. M. McCoy acted as committee chairman. That the project was so soon and so well realized was a lesson to us all, and particularly to Mason, in the durability of Norfolk's "can-do" approach to its challenges.

4

Opening Salvos

THE DEDICATION CEREMONY for the Medical Tower on January 14, 1961 drew a large crowd of public officials, professional personnel, and interested citizens eager to celebrate the completion of Norfolk's handsome new building rising on land recently cleared by the Norfolk Redevelopment and Housing Authority.

At the dedication ceremony, Vincent Kling described the Medical Tower as a new concept for office buildings in Norfolk. He said that redevelopment as reflected in the medical center and Norfolk's massive urban renewal program would offer architects and municipal planners a very great opportunity over the next two decades. He also said that if Norfolk reached its potential as the leading East Coast port, the population would increase dramatically and there would be great need for many more doctors.

Mason spoke of the need for convenient access to the medical center greater than that provided by existing routes going east and south. Saying that it would directly affect the center's usefulness, he proposed a limited access road to the center through a new Portsmouth tunnel, continuing through or around downtown Norfolk, and on to Virginia Beach. He addressed the difficult decision in allocating limited resources facing elected officials, but observed that when these limited resources are spent

Architect's rendering of Medical Tower

on inadequate solutions it becomes necessary to replace or parallel them. He also suggested that a citizens' planning commission, similar to those in Philadelphia, Baltimore, and Pittsburgh, which could study and make recommendations on an objective, scientific basis, might be useful to elected officials.

Mason would speak about road access on many occasions to follow, but today's traffic tie-ups speak of inadequate solutions. However, the city's Department of Planning would be completely reorganized — very probably with the guidance of Vincent Kling, who was working on the design of Norfolk's city hall complex — and, in January 1963, Mason would be sworn in as one of the seven members of the newly formed Norfolk Planning Commission.

The memorable occasion was concluded with accolades from Bill Gilbane; from Mr. Thomas P. Murray of the Equitable Life Insurance Society, holder of a $1.8 million mortgage on the building; and from the City in the form of a citation for contribution to the business, social, and cultural life of the city, presented to Mason Andrews by Norfolk City Councilman Roy B. Martin, Jr.

But before the ceremony concluded there came the talk that most directly bears on this tale — Larry Cox's proposal to expand ambitions for the medical center to include a school of medicine. "What two years ago was expressed as hope," he declared, "is now to me an anticipation."

5

MAKING THE CASE FOR A MEDICAL SCHOOL

LARRY COX HAD DONE MUCH careful research into the need for a medical school, and his suggestion was being favorably received throughout the broader community. Now it was time to solidify support for the idea within both the medical and lay communities. Drawn to the project by his recent happy experience with the Medical Tower and a passionate conviction that uncounted generations could truly benefit by a school striving for the academic and scientific excellence he'd known at Johns Hopkins, Mason became a dedicated activist.

I think it accurate to say that in the 1960's, the medical community was generally in agreement that medical education in eastern Virginia was in a deplorable condition. Problems with residency programs were cited repeatedly. Local physicians were encouraged by the medical society and hospital staff to devote time to hospital teaching, but met with only minimal success.

Deeply affected by the residency education crises were patients not only in Hampton Roads, but also from a large segment of northeastern North Carolina who came to Norfolk, primarily, for their medical care. A school of medicine could bring a higher caliber of medical resident attracted to the educational opportunities it would offer, thereby improv-

Drs. Andrews, Leymaster and Powers assess feasibility of a Norfolk medical school for AMA — February, 1962

ing care in area hospitals and, eventually, in private practices as well.

In order to address the residency program problems, it was sometimes necessary to help key laymen understand the realities of the situation. Even a visionary like Mr. Kaufman asked why the extant residency program needed to be changed. Mason answered by asking where Mr. Kaufman himself went for treatment for his heart condition. When Mr. Kaufman answered that he went to Duke, he had also answered his own question.

But not only was the local residency program unsatisfactory, the state of medicine generally was far from cutting edge. This was generally recognized within the medical community. In April 1961, only a few short months after Larry Cox's speech at the Medical Tower dedication, the Norfolk County Medical Society endorsed the idea of a medical school in Norfolk. To understand how to begin to execute the idea it had endorsed, Mason, its president, appointed a committee to study the proposal.

The society then invited the views of two authorities regarding requirements for starting a medical school. In February 1962, Dr. Glenn Leymaster from the American Medical Association and Dr. Lee Powers of the AMA's Liaison Committee on Medical Education made a preliminary visit to Norfolk and toured the local medical facilities, including the U.S. Naval Hospital in Portsmouth. Their report was generally favorable to the idea that a need for a medical school existed in eastern Virginia and that clinical facilities were adequate to support one. However, they expressed some concern about what they saw as the inadequacy of institutions of higher education with which a medical school might partner, and suggested a broader survey of medical education in Virginia.

Hampton Roads was the largest population center in the United States without a medical school. This fact was attested to in a brochure, copies of which were always available in the pockets of Mason Andrews. Almost daily he passed out his tracts to anyone willing to stand still long enough to hear his pitch for a medical school in eastern Virginia:

1. A school of medicine would contribute enormously to the economy and quality of life in the area

2. A school of medicine would help alleviate the looming shortage of doctors in the United States.

It took Virginia Governor Linwood Holton to point out to Mason, years later, that there was no date on the brochure, which might lead some readers to question the currency of the data cited.

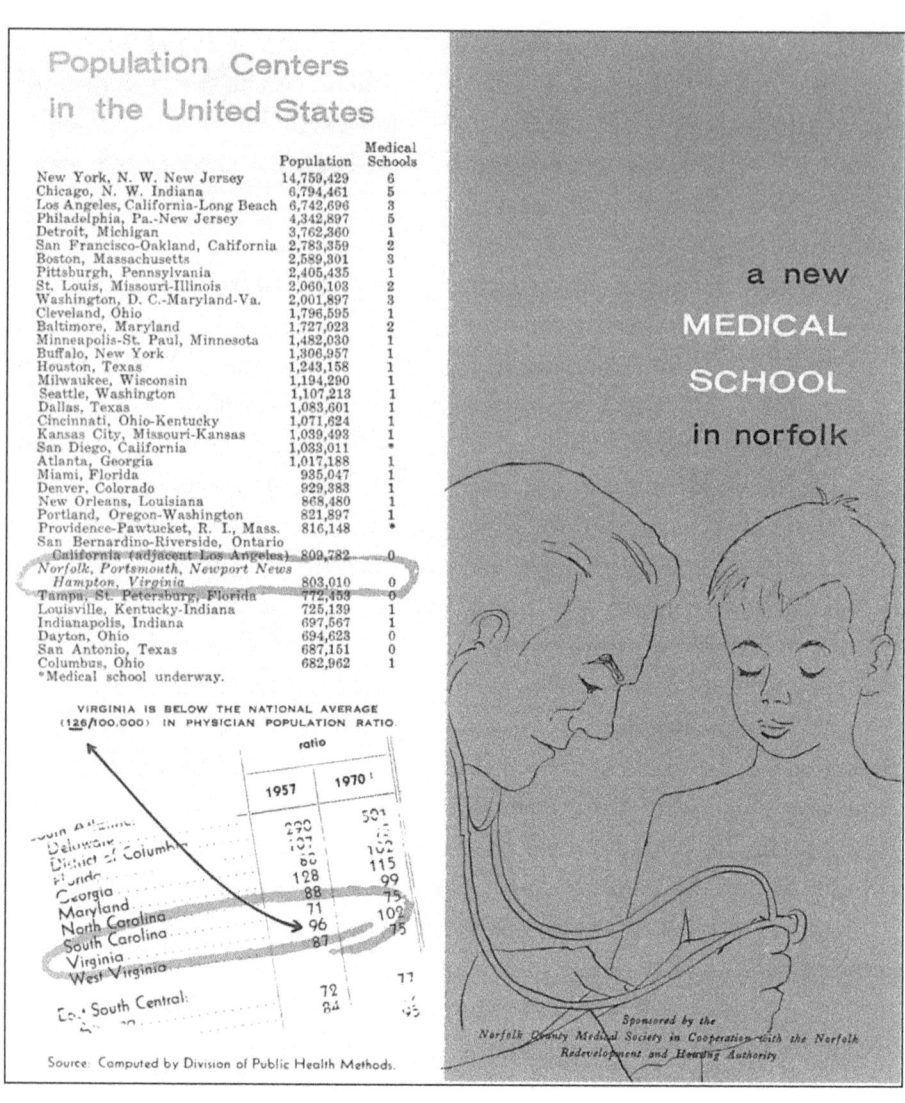

Mason Andrews' early brochure for the medical school

6

IN SEARCH OF A
DESIGNATED DRIVER

AT NRHA, LARRY COX HAD received a number of requests for land in the center from a variety of health-related entities. For assistance in determining which requests it would be appropriate to authorize for inclusion, Larry Cox turned to Norfolk's Health, Welfare, and Recreation Planning Council.

The Planning Council, comprised of a professional planning staff and a citizen board, was engaged primarily in the study of requests from health, welfare, and recreation services for inclusion in the United Way budget. As discussed in the first chapter, the United Way's success had long been a Norfolk priority. George Rice was the Planning Council's executive director. A number of Planning Council board members were destined to fill key roles in the establishment of a medical school in Norfolk — Richard F. Welton III; Harry B. Price, Jr.; Mason; Roy R. Charles; John Franklin; and Harry H. Mansbach, to name a few.

As it turned out, the request from NRHA involved a degree of physical planning beyond the scope of the Planning Council's operations. However, a committee of the Planning Council undertook, in October 1962, to consider how planning the medical center should be addressed. In February 1963, it recommended petitioning Norfolk City Council to fund a comprehensive study for planning the medical center. Joining the Planning Council in petitioning the city were the Norfolk County Medical Society, the Norfolk City Planning Commission, the Norfolk Redevelopment and Housing Authority, and the Tidewater Dental Association.

To consider the advantages of a planned approach to the medical center, Larry Cox and Mason assembled a large group of local professionals involved in health organizations together with a team of experts in health and medical center planning. A steering committee, the Medical Center Commission, was formed and began to consider, among other things, a master plan for the medical center.

During this time, various grant applications for planning funds made by the Planning Council did not receive favorable responses, primarily because the Medical Center Commission was a volunteer organization. To remedy this, the Medical Center Commission asked the Norfolk City Council in January 1964 to petition the Virginia General Assembly to make the Medical Center Commission a public authority by law.

In these early faltering steps toward organization, good will and enthusiasm were high. Despite the enormity of the task being considered and the participants' lack of specific training in many aspects of the undertaking, the conviction seemed to settle in that the project was not only possible but also a goal that would be realized. That success would be achieved and momentum continue to build is perhaps best summed up by the coined phrase of one participant during this era as he looked to the future: "We'll be rowing down the Rubicon with all flags flying."

7

CITY AND STATE HELP IN EARLY ORGANIZATION

NORFOLK CITY COUNCIL — with Roy Martin serving as its mayor since 1962 — had previously appointed an eight-member medical school advisory committee in April 1963. Known as the Mayor's Advisory Committee on the Establishment of a Medical School in Norfolk, it was chaired by Barron F. Black, a Norfolk attorney. Other committee members included Larry Cox; J. Warren White, Jr., a delegate to the Virginia General Assembly; Mason Andrews; Judge Walter A. Page; Dr. John S. Thiemeyer, Jr.; J. Hoge Tyler III, Seaboard Bank president; and Lewis W. Webb, President of Old Dominion College.

The Norfolk County Medical Society had endorsed the establishment of a medical school in 1961. That same year, the Committee on Medical Education of the Medical Society of Virginia had reported the impending national need for more doctors and concluded that an unusual and unique opportunity to help meet that need seemed to exist in Norfolk.

With the involvement of Warren White furthering the cause of the proposed school, a saga began on the home front which is vividly remembered by Mason's children today. Both Warren and Mason attended the same church – First Presbyterian – at the corner of Colonial and Redgate avenues. The fervor of Mason's lobbying out on the sidewalk for the state's support of the school may have exceeded the religious fervor transpiring inside the building. In the words of one of our daughters:

> Every Sunday afternoon my sister and I, having sat still and tried to think good thoughts as long as two children can possibly be expected to do, would bend all possible efforts to getting Daddy to the car to take us home. I suspect Warren White probably also dreamed of such hasty departures. None of us ever succeeded. They stood on the sidewalk in front of the church for what in little-girl time was weeks on end. No whining, wheedling, tugging or pleading could distract Daddy from lobbying. Eventually Warren White introduced and saw through a bill authorizing the study and funding, no doubt in part fuelled by nostalgia for hot Sunday dinners.

Indeed in 1962, Warren White drafted, and the General Assembly passed, legislation directing the State Council of Higher Education to undertake a study of the feasibility of establishing a medical school in Hampton Roads. The State Council's statewide committee included Mason. In January 1964, the committee released a comprehensive report stating that it would be feasible and desirable to establish a private, four-year medical school in Hampton Roads.

The enthusiastic response of Advisory Committee Chairman Barron Black to the statewide study report included the following statement as reported in the local press:

> A project of this magnitude and human importance must be accomplished with excellence if at all. This area — the largest population center in the United States without a medical school — is endowed with the prerequisites important to a school of medicine to a degree possibly unmatched elsewhere. The only remaining requirement is a commitment for an endowment to yield $1 million annually by 1971 and $1.5 million annually by 1975.

The magnitude of philanthropy required may well be judged to be far exceeded by the magnitude of human benefits which would surely flow from the chain of events it would set in motion. ...The benefits would be multiplied many-fold as they continue to be generated throughout the foreseeable future.

Delegate J. Warren White's legislative activities have provided the authority for the studies which produced the favorable report ... and ... it is eminently proper to say that the dynamic spirit behind the proposed new medical college in Norfolk is Dr. Mason C. Andrews. His labors have been largely responsible for the favorable outcome of the matter.

Chairman Black thanked many individuals' and organizations constructive interest and support, mentioning specifically the Norfolk County Medical Society, Norfolk General Hospital, DePaul Hospital, Norfolk City Council, and Portsmouth Academy of Medicine. "Without the appropriation of funds ($1,000 for expenses) and encouragement and the support of Norfolk City Council, no progress at all would have been made."

The report of the Council of Higher Education indicated the need for $35 million in endowment funds. The mayor's committee set the figure at $33 million. Chairman Black indicated that "if $25 million were available now and left to accumulate in a tax-free medical foundation, there would be provided sufficient funds by 1975 when the school is expected to be in full operation."

Delegate White said that he was optimistic that "on the basis of the favorable report, various private foundations will show interest in committing funds to the school."

8

EXPERT ADVICE NETS A HUNTING LICENSE

IN 1963 AND 1964, THE 16-member Medical Center Commission was busy on a number of fronts. It was attempting to plan the medical complex and was seeking funding for its activities. In order to be sure that all opinions and insights available were explored fully, its meetings occasionally included other members of the medical and community leadership. It was committed to seeking and using the most knowledgeable advice available.

Dr. Charles Horton of Norfolk had been a visiting professor of plastic surgery at the University of Missouri School of Medicine. He was acquainted with Dr. Vernon E. Wilson, the dean there. Charlie reportedly told Vernon that Norfolk wanted a medical school but did not know how to start one, and asked him for help. At Mason's invitation, Vernon, an expert on medical school planning, came to Norfolk, reportedly telling colleagues, "There's a fellow down in Norfolk who wants to start a medical school. I'm going down there to look over the situation." Thus began a decade of freely-given and also invaluable advice and guidance.

When Vernon went "down there" on many subsequent occasions, he flew his own single-engine airplane. Once, after a two-day meeting at Virginia Beach, he was urged to spend the night at the Andrews home as he had done before, with the promise of an early-morning start when he was rested. "I need to be in Kansas City early in the morning," he explained, "but I promise you that if I get sleepy, I'll put down in Louisville."

In 1964, Vernon was appointed consultant for technical planning by the Medical Center Commission. He was an incredibly vital — no, essential — factor in the realization of the medical school. As Charlie said of Vernon, "He told us how to go about starting a medical school, step by step." Mason would later say, "Everything that was done was first filtered through the mind of Vernon Wilson." Warm personal memories of Vernon and Ula Wilson are fond recollections, together with the recognition that personal competence seems to beget an attractive modesty.

Dr. Mason Andrews and Dr. Charles Horton confer

THE ARCHITECTURAL SUB-COMMITTEE of the commission, which included Pretlow Darden, John Franklin and Mason, was charged with recommending the firm that would guide the physical form and planning of the center. They did their homework, compiling a list of national architectural firms that might be appropriate for the job here, and consulted with the designer of the acclaimed Kansas City Medical Center. Ultimately they recommended engaging Vincent Kling of Philadelphia to develop the master plan for the complex and to act as architectural consultant. Vincent, beyond his many professional qualifications, was already familiar with local efforts to plan the center through his work as architect for the Medical Tower and the Norfolk civic center.

In January 1964, Mason recommended that the Commission expend $10,000 to finance the initial cost of the master plan. Vincent Kling had estimated a cost of $25,000 to $50,000 for architectural services. By that date, the Commission had received grants totaling $10,500, principally from the Norfolk County Medical Society and the Norfolk Foundation.

It was clear to the Commission members and others that a legally authorized body was needed to facilitate planning of the health services for the center and to develop the school which the State Council of Higher Education said should exist. It was equally apparent that such a legal entity would be necessary for successful fundraising.

The Medical Center Commission urged Norfolk City Council to propose passage of such legislation to the Virginia General Assembly. Re-enter Delegate Warren White to prepare, propose, and guide such legislation.

Warren's warm and friendly manner — as well as his political skills — were unquestionably assets in this venture, an ambitious one for a relatively new member of the House of Delegates. Among the obstacles he faced was the powerful opposition of the state's two existing medical schools (The University of Virginia School of Medicine and the Medical College of Virginia), fearful that a third school might diminish their state funding. Governor Albertis Harrison was also opposed to a third school for fear that it would become a responsibility of the state if local support waned.

Without Warren's strong commitment to the idea of a medical school in Norfolk and his friendly and convincing pursuit of it in the legislature, the passage of the desired legislation might have been impossible.

Guy Friddell, a newspaper columnist of usually humorous fare for the *Virginian-Pilot* in Norfolk, was also an observer and reporter of most things political in Richmond. On the historic day of Warren's final plea to his colleagues for passage of the proposed legislation, Guy Friddell reported that as Warren answered questions about the legislation, he was moved to say, "Aw, c'mon fellows, this is a good thing."

The legislation was passed and signed into law by Governor Harrison, creating the Norfolk Area Medical Center Authority, NAMCA, in March 1964.

On Mason's return from Richmond that day I asked if he'd succeeded in getting any funding from the state. "No," he replied, "what we got was a hunting license."

9

THE NAMCA TEAM GOES TO WORK

THE MEDICAL CENTER COMMISSION, which had been in existence for less than a year, had made important strides in planning for the medical center. But when the Virginia General Assembly authorized the creation of Norfolk Area Medical Center Authority (NAMCA), Toy D. Savage, who was then serving as chairman of the Medical Center Commission, suggested that the Commission disband. He proposed that the Commission turn over its planning documents and funds to the new Authority. The turnover was made promptly to facilitate organization of the new Authority. Toy Savage stated in a press interview that "...whether the final scope of the medical center is large or small, it will certainly be better if its inevitable growth will be in accordance with an overall plan. It is important that each new addition foster rather than deter the next."

Norfolk City Council, which had supported the medical school effort and the legislation to create NAMCA, acted as appointing agent for the Authority. The majority of the citizens appointed to the seven-person Authority were already deeply involved in the work of the disbanding Medical Center Commission. Toy Savage, Mason, and John Franklin were appointed for three-year terms. Roy Charles and Larry Cox were appointed for two-year terms. Judge Page, a former president of DePaul Hospital, and R. R. Richardson, president of Norfolk General Hospital, were appointed for one-year terms.

At the second organizational meeting of NAMCA on June 2, 1964, Mason was elected chairman, and Toy Savage was elected permanent vice-chairman from the slate presented by John Franklin, chairman of the nominating committee. George Rice, Executive Director of the Health, Welfare and Recreation Planning Council was enlisted as secretary-treasurer, and early meetings were held in the Planning Council offices.

Dr. John Franklin

Mason was quoted in a *Virginian-Pilot* news article on June 4, 1964, as saying that the evolution of a projected one hundred million dollar medical center here "is a complicated and sensitive task. It can be done only if the medical and civic talent is able to work constructively together," adding that "the Authority can serve as a catalyst to coordinate the effort." "The opportunity to build upon the excellent progress already made by many groups and individuals is enormous and compelling," he concluded. Mason the leader would always give credit to the team accomplishment, and indeed appropriately so.

10

Portrait of a Leader

AT THIS POINT IN THE STORY Mason had been hard at work on the cause of the school for a few years, but there were even more years ahead. The goals were audacious; the challenge of the work would have dampened the commitment of many. As Mason seemed to be committed to continuing his efforts as agitator-in-chief, it might occur to readers to wonder more about what drove him and why others continued to unite behind the effort with him. A few vignettes, then, on what the family observed of the man, for whatever insights they may offer.

Mason's obstetrician father was a business and civic example for his son. In Dr. C. J. Andrews' effort to have Norfolk's milk supply pasteurized, he incurred the displeasure of the mayor, who was his neighbor. The mayor threatened to keep a cow in his yard unless the project was abandoned. But the scientific evidence in favor of pasteurization was sound, and it prevailed. Presumably the mayor learned to drink pasteurized milk.

The schoolboy Mason was conservative of speech. When asked by a visitor about his reticence, he is said to have replied, "Mother talks and 'Nonnie' talks, but I only talk when I have something to say." Not much changed over time — very little small talk, but passionate advocacy for those dreams of making things better in the city he loved.

On the home front, Mason liked to say, "We're all in this thing together." What followed frequently was an opinion adjustment on the part of a family member. "This thing" could be the choice of a movie on a rare free evening, or it could concern something he liked to term "the right thing to do." The Andrews daughters still quote, with some feeling, the oft-heard, irritatingly inarguable reason for deferring some pleasure or undertaking an unappealing activity. Whatever he wanted done or not done was necessary, he said, "for your future happiness and in the long run," or "it will build your character."

Dr. Mason Andrews

Mason's patient and respectful, but persistent civic leadership involved assembling a strong team to address a perceived issue, seeking all pertinent information and opinion, weighing it thoroughly, and reaching a conclusion seeking the greatest good — and then promoting a plan, sometimes referred to as "an impossible dream."

The conclusions were not always immediately enthusiastically embraced, but they tended to prevail when thoughtfully tested.

Later in his career, in a profile Guy Friddell published in the *Virginian-Pilot*, Mason's friend Henry Hunter was quoted as saying, "Sometimes it seems like I've spent all my life listening to Mason explain something that had to be done if the city was going to survive."

His family and many colleagues did, indeed, sometimes weary of the calls to arms, but they always knew that his conclusions were logically sound and unselfishly motivated. Sometimes, to absorb more of the thought process leading to the conclusion, however, there was need to have him idle down that thought engine and let everyone else recognize his vision.

That was the way things usually turned out, and the result was a team, committed to the plan and ready to promote it. Mason gave credit for success to team effort, and indeed it was so. Team members tended to be successful citizens in their own fields of endeavor. Even so, they may have surprised even themselves as they overcame incredible obstacles to realization of "the impossible dream."

Over the course of the many years of his civic activities, Mason's notion of teamwork was refined into what he called The Process. The Process consisted of assembling "everyone around the same table at the same time." "Everyone" meant board, staff, the best possible consultants, and others as appropriate for "everyone to be on the same page" at all times. He believed that The Process was, in fact, the easiest and most direct path to the desired result and that it tended to eliminate costly problems "down the road." It seemed so simple to follow The Process — it simply required integrity of motivation and respect for the advice of the best other voices. He argued that it led consistently to achievement.

His vision, motivation, and powers of persuasion were extraordinary. There was an intensity and persistence about his pursuit of a goal, and always the integrity of purpose and the pursuit of excellence that were his hallmarks.

Mason liked to quote (actually misquote) architect Daniel Burnham as: "Make no small plans. They have no power to stir men's minds." (More accurately, "Make no little plans. They have no magic to stir men's blood, and probably not themselves be realized. Make big plans; aim high in hope and work. ...") He took this dictum to heart, and his bold planning delivered valuable assets for the city he loved.

II

THE MEDICAL CENTER MOTEL

THE MULTITUDE OF TASKS and decisions to be addressed by NAMCA, seemingly simultaneously, was daunting. That the goal of a medical school in Norfolk could have been reached by NAMCA's deeply committed citizen team, led by a practicing obstetrician/gynecologist, is remarkable. And while the time, talent and effort expended before NAMCA's creation had been enormous, the work and its fallout would jump exponentially during the coming era.

The Andrews office and home front became accustomed to seeing flying coattails and stacks of callback messages. Mason's brother, Dr. William C. Andrews, who had also joined their father's medical practice, in 2008 described his role in the establishment of the medical school as follows: "I back-stopped Mason when he had to go to Richmond." At their office, Mason's patients continued to exhibit commendable patience as they waited. At home, overly optimistic time-of-arrival goals were dealt with philosophically. It was exasperating at times, but on both fronts it seemed to develop the essential trait of forbearance, by and large.

All consultants were meeting with NAMCA regularly to formulate the best courses of action. At this point the group included Dr. Richardson K. Noback, Executive Director of the Kansas City General

Hospital and Medical Center and Associate Dean of the University of Missouri School of Medicine. Dr. Noback had been Dr. Vernon Wilson's inspired suggestion. Dr. Noback, an expert in medical education, became NAMCA's Executive Medical Consultant, joining Vincent Kling who was Executive Architectural Consultant.

Dr. Richardson K. Noback

The consultants who honored the Andrews family with their after-hours presence were an impressive group during the founding years of the medical school, as well as in subsequent endeavors undertaken by Mason. These guests, including two who later occupied covers of *Time* magazine, appeared to enjoy these interludes in lieu of hotel stays, and NAMCA's finite monetary resources were spared a little bit of strain. In addition to their expert advice to NAMCA, freely given, they became cherished friends.

As one Andrews daughter later described life on the home front, "Daddy lifted his wife and young children up from the vast ranks of the unemployed, retraining them for productive careers in the hospitality industry."

Another Andrews daughter confessed that as a child she did not know the meaning of the word "consultant." She wondered, "Who are these people? And why do they keep coming back?"

On a return trip from summer camp the family spent a night in a motel, the first time for these little girls. They instantly saw a similarity with activity on the home front: people came; they spent the night; they had breakfast; they went on their way. Soon after, this sign was posted by them in the Andrews' guest room closet:

Welcome to the
MEDICAL CENTER MOTEL
Established 1958
Under Family Management

A favorite "regular" who became regarded as almost a family member was Dick Noback. He would join the schoolchildren and their mother (their father frequently departing earlier to do some task required by his primary job) at the breakfast table. His approach was announced by an interesting interface between his crepe-soled shoes and the slate hallway floor. The children would exchange glances and then announce, "Here comes Squeaky Shoes." Dick and Nan Noback became cherished

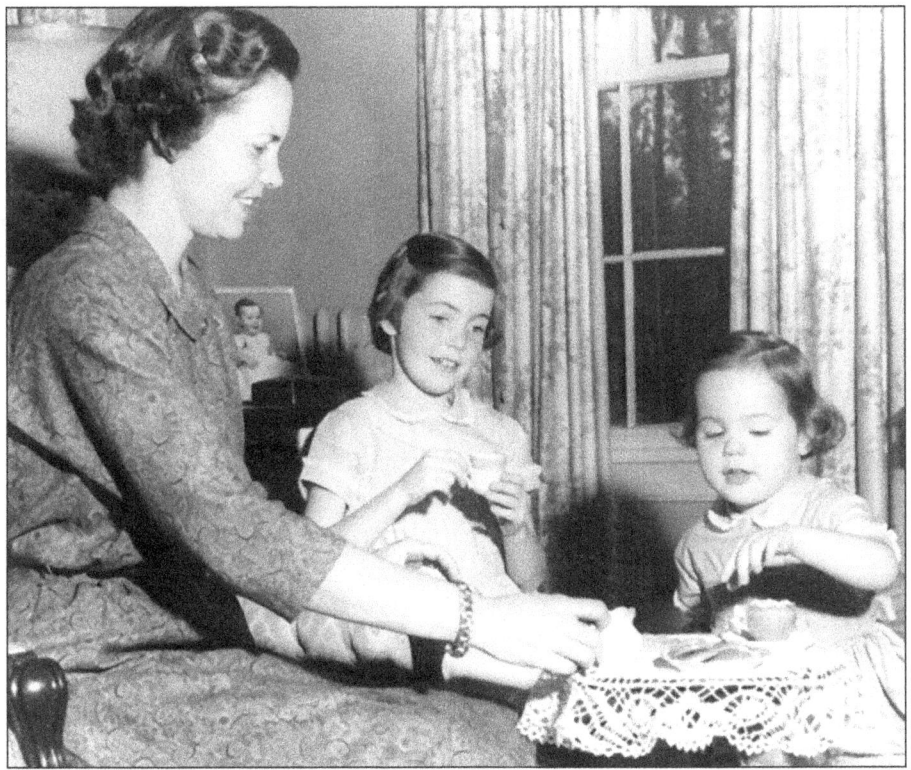

Sabine, Jean and Mason Andrews, 1957

family friends and our children became acquainted. Dick's loyalty extends even to today with gracious assistance with this story.

So seemed the hubbub on the home front. Mason's view of 1964 is recorded in a 1984 timeline recalling the steps to founding the school:

> Precise planning documents including goals and steps toward achieving a medical center and medical school prepared by Noback and adopted by Authority. Physical plans including expansion of medical center, east and south, designed by Kling. Medical Advisory Committee headed by Dr. Robert L. Payne [Jr.] began regular productive meetings. Lay Advisory Committee formed including most of the recognized civic leaders. Initial meeting addressed by Nathan Stark, President of Kansas City Medical Center and Executive Vice President of Hallmark Cards emphasized the importance of teaching and research to the quality of medical care in an environment.

12

DR. ANDREWS GOES TO WASHINGTON

IN ADDITION TO PONDERING how to reach a $35 million endowment goal, there was an immediate need to fund staff and expenses.

In December 1964, Mason, accompanied by Toy Savage, R. R. Richardson, and Larry Cox, asked Norfolk City Council to provide $231,400 over a three-year period to NAMCA to complete its planning. Mayor Martin was encouraging, as he foresaw the enormous financial benefits to the city, apart from the medical advantages, should NAMCA's goals be realized. City Manager Thomas Maxwell recommended that the council approve the appropriation with the proviso that the money would not continue to be disbursed if funds became available from another source.

In 1965, the federal government under President Lyndon Johnson was encouraging the development of regional medical complexes in Virginia and other states. The aim was to have centers readily accessible to treat heart, stroke, and cancer patients. Bills dealing with this idea were being considered in both houses of Congress.

Mason, as chairman of NAMCA, along with Dr. Kinloch Nelson, Dean of the Medical College of Virginia, and Dr. Kenneth R. Crispell, Dean of the University of Virginia School of Medicine, testified jointly before the House Commerce Committee that planning should be done on a statewide basis. It was noted that NAMCA's planned medical school in Norfolk "will be privately endowed." It must be acknowledged that such an endowment at the time was entirely theoretical.

In a separate statement, Mason said that in Norfolk, federal funds being considered for development of regional medical complexes would be an important supplement to funds derived from state and private sources.

In an interview after the hearing, Mason spoke with the *Virginian-Pilot*'s Washington reporter Luther J. Carterand addressing several points of interest:

• He forecast that NAMCA's operating debt would be $400,000 by 1968 when all major components of the medical center, except the medical school, were expected to be in place; $1 million by 1971 when the medical school was expected to open; and $1.5 million by 1975 when the school was expected to be fully developed.

• He noted that federal funds might cover as much as one-third of the debt.

• He addressed the two different pieces of legislation concerning the disbursement of such federal funds. The Senate had already passed legislation authorizing grants of up to $150 million over the next four years. The House version authorized $50 million for the first year and "such sums as may be necessary" for each of the succeeding four years. In earlier testimony that day, Mason had asked the House Committee to consider adopting the Senate's version, which did not require a medical school to be open if other facilities such as hospitals were involved in postgraduate medical education. Norfolk might find itself ineligible for federal assistance during the life of the program if a medical school were a requirement. On the other hand, the House version was preferable to the Senate's because it would allow grants of up to ninety percent of the construction costs.

• Mason included, as was his constant reiteration, that Norfolk was a population center of a million residents, the largest such population concentration nationally not served by a medical school.

• He also addressed the necessity of each school's maintaining its autonomy and independence. "Their individual capacity to exploit, invent and demonstrate is fundamental to progress," he said.

The report closes with Mason's observation that "the medical school can get under way when a private endowment of from $10 million to $15 million has been established."

IT WAS, PERHAPS, THE ACTIVITY involved in hunting such an endowment that kept Mason from accepting an invitation by President Johnson to attend the signing of the medical complex bill on Wednesday, October 6, 1965 at the White House.

13

IN SEARCH OF AN ACADEMIC AFFILIATION

PLANNING FOR A MEDICAL SCHOOL in Norfolk presented multiple issues, all of which seemed to be clamoring for attention simultaneously.

NAMCA approached problem solving with all the expert advice it could muster. Adding to Vernon Wilson, Dick Noback, and Vincent Kling, NAMCA created an advisory committee of respected and able local citizens in business, industry and the professions to help it thread its way along the obstacle course stretching before it. William P. Woodley chaired the committee composed of State Senator Edward L. Breeden, Drs. William F. Murphy, Robert L. Payne, Jr., and Jack C. Kantor, and attorney Harry Mansbach.

One of the pressing issues to be addressed concerned the apparent need for a local institution of higher education with which to join ranks. Most medical schools in the United States were affiliated with a university, and often with a medical school hospital as well. It will be remembered that, on a preliminary visit to Norfolk in 1962, members of the AMA's Liaison Committee on Medical Education had expressed concern about the adequacy of local institutions of higher education. Although Mayor Martin had responded to their concerns by citing Old

Dominion College, Norfolk State College, and the emerging Virginia Wesleyan College as examples of institutions of higher education in the Norfolk area, there did not seem to be an obvious solution to the need for an academic base for a medical school.

Because the State Council of Higher Education, in its 1964 study of the feasibility of establishing a medical school in Hampton Roads, had articulated that it would probably be necessary for the proposed medical school to affiliate with Old Dominion College (ODC) or another state-supported institution of higher education, exploration with ODC seemed the logical first step. In fact, an affiliation between the proposed medical school and ODC became a local assumption. But when a *Virginian-Pilot* editorial on December 7, 1964 mentioned that "the M.D. degree would be granted by ODC." Frank Batten, Chairman of the ODC Advisory Board, is said to have received a telephone call from Governor Harrison the same day. The Governor's message was, in essence, "Stop." Governor Harrison was opposed to a third medical school in Virginia because he feared that it would become a state responsibility if it lost its local support.

NAMCA officials met at length with ODC officials to address the options and problems of affiliation. A joint liaison committee was established in 1965 which included Frank Batten and Lewis Webb, President of ODC and, for NAMCA, Mason, Roy Charles, John Franklin, Harry Mansbach, Walter Page, Bob Payne, Harry Price, and Dick Welton.

Dick Noback was often involved in discussions, as was Vernon Wilson, each step proceeding with their knowledge and advice. ODC also had its own consultants study the issue of affiliation with the proposed medical school. Their recommendations were, basically, that the medical school would provide the funding, that it would become a division of ODC, and that NAMCA would fill an advisory role in the operation of the medical school.

ODC was committed to its undergraduate program, and although it had begun designing its basic science programs with a medical school in mind it would be the late 1970's before it would be in a position to offer necessary courses for a medical school program. NAMCA did not want to delay the opening of the proposed medical school beyond 1972. In addition to this problem, Dr. Lewis Webb, president of ODC, was opposed to any affiliation with a medical school for fear it would compromise the undergraduate program. This left the negotiations at a temporary impasse.

Another academic center to be approached early on was the College of William and Mary in Williamsburg. Williamsburg is approximately fifty miles from Norfolk. William and Mary had a long academic relationship with Norfolk: The Norfolk Division of the College of William and Mary had only recently been spun off as Old Dominion College when the local student body outgrew the parent institution. Cordial exploration continued for several years between NAMCA and William and Mary authorities, but never progressed beyond preliminary talks.

Later, when Dr. Thomas Moore was being recruited as a possible dean for Eastern Virginia Medical School, he stated that he would only be interested in being dean of the William and Mary Medical School. Tom Moore produced a photograph of a Dr. McClurg who had been Chairman of Medicine at William and Mary before Thomas Jefferson moved on to Charlottesville with certain academic assets. This, Dr. Moore pointed out, made the William and Mary School of Medicine the "first medical school in America," thus pre-dating Harvard Medical School.

A possible relationship with the Medical College of Virginia (MCV) affiliated with Virginia Commonwealth University in Richmond had also been explored. MCV had expressed strong opposition to a third medical school in Virginia when the Virginia legislature was considering the request of the Norfolk Medical Commission for legal status. The fear of both state medical schools was that they might lose some of their state funding, which was already inadequate, to a third school. Although talks did not lead to a proposed affiliation, Dr. Kinloch Nelson, Dean of the Medical College of Virginia, continued to be cordial and helpful in talks with NAMCA.

Another possibility for affiliation seemed to be with the University of Virginia in Charlottesville. The University of Virginia was already on record, with MCV, as opposing a third medical school in Virginia for fear this might jeopardize its funding. But this did not necessarily preclude some sort of academic affiliation, and the talks proceeded with energy. When it became apparent that the University's terms would be for basic science years to take place in Charlottesville with clinical science years taking place in Norfolk, the arrangement sent the NAMCA team scurrying for consultation with even more experts.

NAMCA had by then acquired its first executive officer, Admiral H. Page Smith, USN (Ret.). Page Smith had just retired as Supreme Allied Commander Atlantic (SACLANT). This lovely gentleman, who could spin exciting sea stories and could also grow magnificent roses, had just a few weeks earlier been attended by full Navy ceremony and courtesy. Now he found himself flying coach class and carrying Mason's orthopedic seat and slide projector on various trips as they sought funding and advice for NAMCA. One such trip was to consult President Milton Eisenhower at the Johns Hopkins University about the advisability of accepting the University of Virginia's proposal. President Eisenhower commented that this would not actually constitute a medical school. The pleasant conversation concluded with Page Smith's comment: "I have enjoyed playing golf with your brother." This was one of many occasions when busy top-level leaders graciously gave their time and attention when sincerely sought for sound, unselfish causes, with no remuneration asked or expected. Such experiences lent valuable encouragement to NAMCA officials.

It seems now permissible to relate a story which might be called "Yalta on the Chesapeake Bay." In the era of the search for affiliation, there had been a hasty afternoon trip to the Windmill Point Marina aboard our boat despite the usual concern about afternoon storms. Upon arrival, the first mate and guests were invited to go ashore and to make an extended visit to the marina gift shop. Nothing was spelled out, but there was an aura of mystery present. The skipper had guests below-decks but their identity was not revealed. It was, indeed, a clandestine meeting of some moment. If secrecy was pledged, Mason abided by his promise. He never revealed the names of the visitors nor the subject of the meeting. Considering the timing in the context of negotiations with the University of Virginia Medical School, the first mate — in the style of CNN — currently projects the identity of one of the guests as Dr. Ken Crispell, Dean of the University of Virginia Medical School.

It was back to the drawing board with ODC. Even though obstacles had been encountered, ODC officials, including President Lewis Webb, meeting with Dick Noback, had agreed in April 1966 that affiliation between ODC and the proposed medical school should be pursued. Frank Batten, Chairman of the ODC Board of Advisors, stated that the Board endorsed the idea of a medical school in Norfolk and was prepared to enter into an affiliation agreement with NAMCA to develop plans for a medical school. Meetings between members of the Norfolk County Medical Society and NAMCA officials endeavored to assist in the search for an acceptable affiliation process.

After four years, some affiliation with ODC, which became ODU (Old Dominion University) in 1969, seemed to offer the most acceptable prospect.

14

GROWING PAINS – SECURING A SITE

PHYSICAL PLANNING OF THE MEDICAL CENTER was a NAMCA priority. Approximately thirty-five acres of land comprised the medical center in the Atlantic City redevelopment project. The center already included the Norfolk General Hospital, Children's Hospital of The King's Daughters, the Medical Tower, and the Norfolk Public Health Department building.

The million-dollar Regional Comprehensive Rehabilitation Institute, offering advanced physical, speech, hearing, psychological and vocational counseling, and job training, was soon to be built, although not actually in the center, as was being reported in the press. The Institute, a fine addition to the area's health care assets, was being constructed across Brambleton Avenue from the medical center. The Tidewater Health Foundation had responsibility for its planning and construction costs, which were met in part by a federal Hill-Burton matching grant.

A number of proprietary agency requests for land in the center, such as for nursing homes and housing, had apparently been deferred, but the press was mentioning plans for a new research facility, a mental health facility, and a dental institute.

Architect-planner Vincent Kling had offered two versions of a plan for the center during the three years of intense study with NAMCA:

a high-rise option and a campus-style complex.

It was essential that new buildings be arranged in the proper relationship to existing buildings and to future buildings. Kling could see that if a medical school were to be included, more land would be required.

The possibility of locating the medical school off site had to be considered. As discussed in the previous chapter, NAMCA had been exploring options for an academic relationship with an institution of higher education in the region. Neither the University of Virginia nor William and Mary appeared to be the perfect partner, for a variety of reasons mentioned earlier. There was a good deal of uncommitted land adjacent to Old Dominion College, and it was considered to be within a reasonable commute distance of the medical center, approximately one mile. Mason, in line with his philosophy of exploring every option before making a decision, believed it important to consider the possibility of placing the proposed medical school on the ODC campus, and expressed this to Norfolk City Council. In October 1966, however, Frank Batten, Chairman of the ODC Advisory Board, told Norfolk City Council that ODC advisors recommended ODC not be the site of the proposed medical school, citing economic concerns.

There seemed to be real wisdom in placing the medical school in the medical center complex immediately adjacent to its supporting facilities. To do this, however, would require additional land beyond the acreage assembled by NRHA for redevelopment.

To create a cohesive campus for the medical center and school uninterrupted by major thoroughfares, additional land would be needed to the east. The land needed was part of Ghent, a neighborhood of significant houses. Further, it contained most of the neighborhood's commercial development.

An Andrews daughter recalls the troubled mood of her father on the night before a public hearing on the issue. He explained that he was distressed because of the distress that would be caused to people who stood to lose their property and those who would legitimately feel that

View toward Ghent from Medical Center prior to the reconfiguration of Colley Avenue

their neighborhood would be diminished. He concluded that the greater good to be gained for the city and the region made the plan for expansion of the medical center compelling.

Created under the guidance of Vincent Kling, the plan proposed moving Colley Avenue east to encompass the acreage needed for the medical school, 17.69 additional acres. In addition to the issues relating to Ghent, relocating Colley Avenue would be an expensive undertaking for the city.

The public hearing took place on October 11, 1966, before Norfolk City Council. The Council chamber was crowded with proponents and opponents. Attorney J. Hume Taylor represented a newly-formed concerned citizens committee. He expressed for them their complete support for a medical school but pleaded for some plan that would spare their houses and businesses.

Among those speaking for the plan, in addition to Mason for NAMCA, were Bob Payne, representing the medical advisory com-

Architect's model of proposed campus

mittee to NAMCA; Frank Batten, Rector of ODC; Samuel Ames, President of the Norfolk Chamber of Commerce; and former Mayor W. Fred Duckworth representing the Tidewater Virginia Development Council.

Mason spoke of the extensive research made by NAMCA and its consultants into the area requirements for a medical school. He referred to the nationally acknowledged expertise and talent of its executive consultants, Dick Noback and Vincent Kling. It was considered imperative by medical school planners nationally that medical schools be in close proximity to hospitals and not fragmented by traffic. The fifty-one acre center plan being proposed would represent the basic minimum requirement and would in no way represent the ideal. For example, the Kansas City Medical Center occupies an area of 135 acres.

Frank Batten called the plan "workable and reasonable" and said that its adoption would represent "a giant step" toward the establishment of a medical school.

Bob Payne said his committee was "convinced that facilities in the center need to be close together" and that the land required "is not excessive."

Former Mayor Duckworth called the proposed medical school an asset in attracting industry, saying, "We need it, and need it badly."

Sam Ames said the center represented a $100-million industry which would bring to the area "the type of citizen we need and want."

The hope was expressed by a Ghent neighborhood resident that the medical school could manage with less land if high rise construction were utilized, similar to but smaller than MCV (Medical College of Virginia). Mason responded that high-rise construction had been studied and that some high rise would be utilized, depending upon the use of the particular building. He reiterated that the planning had been carefully studied for three years, and that the proposed additional land represented the bare minimum for the buildings required for a medical school. He said that specific requests would be considered by the appropriate NAMCA committees and NAMCA.

Dr. Robert L. Payne, Jr.

Roy B. Martin, Jr.

Probably concerned that the requisite structures would have to be actually squeezed into the total of fifty-one acres, Mason would later say that he hoped the request would not be seen in future years as far too little.

At the end of the two-and-a-half hour public hearing, the Norfolk

City Council adopted the NAMCA request by unanimous vote. Mayor Martin commented, "I hope that no one will feel in future years that a mistake was made here today."

At the hearing Mason had said that at least six new buildings would have to be built in the center in the next six years. The list of which specific facilities were included in that number varied from one news account to the next. Among those mentioned on the day of the public hearing were a comprehensive mental health center, a research building, regional offices and laboratories for the state public health department, another doctors' office building comparable to the Medical Tower, an addition to the Children's Hospital of The King's Daughters, and an extended care facility.

Efforts to secure a mental health facility in the medical center had been led by State Senator Edward Breeden as chairman of a committee appointed by NAMCA in response to a request by local mental health professionals to study the possibilities and advisability of estab-

Eastern Virginia Medical School has launched a major renovation project for Fairfax Hall, completely refacing the exterior and renovating the interior. When renovations are complete, the building will be renamed the Dr. Mason C. Andrews Hall.

lishing a comprehensive mental health institute in the newly expanded medical center. Dr. Robert H. Barnes of the Kansas City Mental Health Foundation, a consultant to NAMCA's mental health committee, suggested that such a facility would make NAMCA eligible for construction funds under the Community Mental Health Centers Construction Act.

The Virginia General Assembly provided $325,000 to the Authority to be used as matching funds. The federal Hill-Burton plan provided approximately $1.1 million. Over $730,000 was raised locally. The 63,000-square-foot, 80-bed comprehensive Mental Health Center and Psychiatric Institute was completed in 1973 on land conveyed by Norfolk Redevelopment and Housing Authority (NRHA) when Harry Mansbach served as NAMCA's second chairman.

As it happens, the building that was built to house this cutting-edge health facility on Fairfax Avenue is being rebuilt for a second life on campus. After extensive renovation it is to be re-opened as Andrews Hall in Spring 2009.

15

Picking Up the Tab

As ambitious as were the plans for a medical school, with no significant single funding and endowment source apparent, the growing conviction that most of the funding would have to be raised locally from individual donors in Hampton Roads can only be described as audacious. And, while the community was not known for its wealth, the determination and talent of citizens proved eventually to be a resource of great depth in securing the needed endowment.

Without question, the very early financial support for medical center planning was indispensable. Several individuals and organizations contributed greatly needed encouragement and financial support for operating expenses. Of special note were the grants made by the Norfolk City Council, Norfolk County Medical Society, the Norfolk Foundation, and the Oscar F. Smith Foundation. As the idea of a medical school gained acceptance, other important contributions and grants were forthcoming. State and federal support was sought, with modest success as previously stated. For some time, Norfolk City Council was the only municipal body making grants.

It was apparent that several very large grants would be needed if the goal of a medical school in Norfolk were to be reached. Before fundraising was organized in the ultimately successful campaign discussed below, NAMCA members had begun taking note of some of the national philanthropic foundations. And so began a season of taking the cause on the road, usually involving a slide show to underscore compelling arguments and introduce the site and region to those unfamiliar with it.

Creating the slide show, and updating it for each presentation, became part of life on the home front. From a projector perched next to the stove on the kitchen counter, pictures of local facilities were projected onto our refrigerator. The slide sorter, a precarious device, was balanced nearby. It became a serious goal of family members not to jostle this article, thus hoping to avoid being responsible for the total collapse of slides awaiting inclusion in the final production. One man's idea of quality family time was to join the homework and dinner preparation scene, project his slides onto the refrigerator and pause at length between each picture to practice the sales pitch mentally. Everyone learned to duck when passing the refrigerator but sometimes it became necessary to actually open the door if food were to be prepared. This failed to discourage the producer of this documentary, who later would manage to coordinate a sound track for a really high-tech production.

On one such road show, the naïve but purposeful Mason and

One man and a slide projector set out to start a medical school

Admiral Page Smith, Executive Director of NAMCA, sought a grant from the Mellon Foundation in Pittsburgh. The visitors were politely received, with Page carrying the usual encumbrances for the homemade slide show and Mason sporting his operating room shoes, the appalling condition of which was duly noted. No money was forthcoming from Mellon, but another offer was made. "Dr. Andrews," asked the executives, "would you like to have your shoes shined?" Later, the Mellon Foundation gave the medical school $1 million after a more successful approach by Henry Clay Hofheimer.

NAMCA had been advised by its consultants that it would need to raise $15,000,000 — $10 million for endowment and $5 million for facilities. This was said to be a minimum figure. Dr. Vernon Wilson had suggested $50 million for endowment. A nationally respected fundraising organization had advised NAMCA that the most it could hope to raise locally was $4 million to $5 million. Members of NAMCA, however, thought that advice did not take into account the area's "can-do" spirit.

A leader to harness that spirit was needed. With the help of citizens involved on NAMCA's committees and of citizens not yet closely involved, a brilliant candidate was identified: Porter Hardy, Jr., who was about to retire as United States Congressman, representing the local 2nd District. While they believed their decision to be a great one, it remained to be seen if the congressman could be drafted to serve.

In a special Landmark publication, Guy Friddell of the *Virginian-Pilot* quoted Porter Hardy's account of his recruitment for the job: "Mason invited me to lunch before Thanksgiving 1969 at the Harbor Club, and when I got there I found he also had invited the 25 persons he knew I'd have the hardest time saying no to. I agreed to work on the drive six months, I stayed three years."

Porter was extremely well-liked and respected across eastern Virginia and in Washington. He had done a fine job in Congress. He could be forgiven if he had plans to relax upon retirement. But his hosts had chosen well. His skills and benign influence would be invaluable across the region and in Washington as well.

The group met again a few days later in Mr. Kaufman's board room. Porter always seemed easygoing, but he was not naïve. He told his hosts that they must all be co-chairmen and would have to stretch to make their most generous gifts. Thereupon he presented his own generous pledge and asked for their promises without delay. (This was the genesis of a three-year IRS audit on the Andrews home front, to explain how the taxpayer with such a modest income could claim a charitable contribution so disproportionate to his income.)

A further momentous event took place on Tuesday, December 23, 1969, with the establishment of the Eastern Virginia Medical School Foundation and with the election of its officers. Henry Clay Hofheimer of Norfolk, head of Southern Materials Company, was elected president of the foundation. Henry Clay had also been President of Norfolk General Hospital and had long recognized the need for a medical school to attract superior house officers and other bright young physicians. Sol Rawls of Franklin, head of a petroleum distribution company and a member of several health committees established by the governor, was elected vice-president, and W. Wright Harrison of Virginia Beach, head of Virginia National Bank, was elected secretary-treasurer.

As Chairman of NAMCA, Mason also announced to the press and public a list of those who had agreed to serve as co-trustees with the officers, stunning in the breadth of geography and depth of accomplishment it encompassed: Judge Lawrence I'Anson, Portsmouth, of the Virginia Supreme Court of Appeals; Lloyd Noland, Newport News, whose Noland Company remains a successful distributor of mechanical equipment; Sherwood E. Liles, Jr., Virginia Beach, President of Norfolk Construction Co.; Lucius J. Kellam, Belle Haven, president of a heating oil distribution company; and John L. Roper II, President of Norfolk Shipbuilding and Drydock Corporation.

According to a *Virginian-Pilot* account, Mason announced that the foundation would "receive, manage, and distribute the proceeds from gifts and legacies" and would be "influential in determining the direction and standards" of the school. He said trustees were selected to provide "maximum competence in the management and administration of the resources entrusted to the foundation" and to represent diverse geographical areas. According to the *Pilot*, Mason also announced that

• The foundation itself would not solicit funds. Instead, such activity would be carried out by a separate campaign organization, to be announced very shortly.

• Contributions would be tax-deductible since the foundation was chartered by the state corporation commission as a charitable organization.

• Most of the money for construction and operation would come from federal grants and appropriations. Mason expressed the hope that the urgent national need for more medical personnel would result in even more favorable legislation and appropriations.

• If all facets of the plan succeed, the proposed medical school could be ready to accept its first class of medical students in September 1972. Smith Rogers Hall would be used as an interim school facility, with construction of a medical school building to begin in 1973.

THE FOUNDATION'S NEW HEAD, Henry Clay Hofheimer, was also an extremely valuable member of the now-forming fundraising team. In one memorable instance while walking his dogs on the beach, he encountered Sidney and Frances Lewis of Richmond and persuaded them to provide start-up construction funds for the medical school's first building, now known as Lewis Hall. When influential philanthropic industrialists and business people meet, amazing things can begin to happen.

16

LAUNCH!

ON JANUARY 15, 1970, at the Lake Wright Motor Lodge, Porter Hardy and NAMCA launched the largest fundraising campaign in Tidewater history. The goal was to raise $15,000,000 over the next six years to start the medical school. In addition to about 165 business and professional leaders from across eastern Virginia, the gathering included Senator William B. Spong, Jr., 1st District Representative Thomas M. Downing, 2nd District Representative G. William Whitehurst, and Lawrence M. Cox, then Assistant Secretary of Housing and Urban Development.

Mason, as Chairman of NAMCA, said "the time for building a medical school for Tidewater is now." He expounded upon the many advantages to be gained by the entire region from the proposed Eastern Virginia Medical School to be located in the Norfolk medical complex: "more health care personnel… more and a greater variety of medical talent… new and otherwise unobtainable programs for enlarging the quantity and quality of health care." He said that the private, four-year school would be initially under the authority of NAMCA and would maintain close ties with Old Dominion University, but that it eventually would be operated by the Eastern Virginia Medical School Foundation and that NAMCA would fall away.

Financing for the school was outlined as follows in the *Virginian-Pilot* account of the meeting: half of the $15,000,000 would be raised through public subscription in the eastern Virginia communities affected by the school; the other half would be sought from national foundations and special gifts. A grant of $10 million for construction of new medical schools was expected to be made available by the federal government; Norfolk City Council had agreed to contribute $500,000 with certain conditions; the Virginia General Assembly would be asked to contribute about $1 million in student tuition grants.

Porter Hardy announced seven divisions with specific focus on different types of potential donors, as well as co-chairs coordinating efforts within each of the areas of the region. Harry Price, Leonard R. Strelitz, Bill Woodley, and Dick Welton would seek sponsors; Harry Mansbach, Richard F. Wood, Hunter Hogan, Elbert Stewart and John Angelson were to coordinate approaches to individuals; Wright Harrison and M. Lee Payne would head the corporations division; Henry Clay Hofheimer, Sherwood E. Liles, and Roy Charles were to coordinate application to foundations and national corporations; Drs. Charles J. Devine, Jr. and John Franklin would head the campaign's medical division; Dr. Alexander L. Martone the dental division; while J. Hoge Tyler and Mason were to head the political division.

Local leaders were named co-chairs of efforts within each of the area's communities, including: C.E. Thurston, Jr., for Norfolk; W. F. Magann for Portsmouth; T. Raymond Hassell III for Chesapeake; Shirley T. Holland for Suffolk, Isle of Wight and Southampton counties; and Daniel Hartnell for the Eastern Shore.

What had been outlined, then, was an ambitious coordinated effort bringing together and relying upon the talents of business, professional and political leaders throughout Hampton Roads. If their ambitious goal could be reached, this was the plan and these were the people to make it happen.

Dr. Roger O. Egelberg of the federal Department of Health, Education and Welfare was the guest speaker for the fundraiser. He said the creation of the medical school now was especially important because of the looming doctor shortage in the country. Sixty thousand dollars was pledged on the spot, and ten-year pledge cards accompanied departing guests. A beautiful example of regional cooperation was born that evening.

Also available that day was an elegant brochure prepared to equip the chairmen and co-chairmen with proper literature to help them sell the medical school idea. Well before the launch, a reputable public relations firm in Baltimore had been engaged. Its principal had asked necessary questions to help NAMCA focus on important answers. For example, when he had asked who was in charge of fundraising and it was discovered as a consequence that no one was, and no one wanted to be, then Porter Hardy was recruited.

Also emerging from their work was the EVMS logo design, showing the three tracks that are medical school tradition — teaching, research and patient care — intertwined in the way now so familiar to all in the region.

EVMS logo

Overlooked, however, was the deadline for production of the brochure to fit into the fund drive kick-off date. So while the managing principal from the consulting firm took his family skiing over the Christmas holidays, Mason took his family on assignment to help him finish the copy by press time.

The response to the fund drive was phenomenal. In just thirteen months Porter Hardy and his team had raised $7 million. By the time he finished, the immediate future of the Eastern Virginia Medical School seemed assured.

Fundraising celebration: Porter Hardy, Harry Mansbach, Mason Andrews and Henry Clay Hofheimer – February 14, 1971

17

THE HEART STARTS BEATING

As THE FUND DRIVE'S SUCCESS was building enthusiasm for a medical school over most of the Hampton Roads area, the first steps toward fulfilling the other requirements that could lead to accreditation for a medical school were being taken. And, with so many talented advocates and planners, most remaining pockets of resistance to the school began to sign on with enthusiasm — for the most part.

For example, several people exercised their persuasive skills in an attempt to win the support of Norfolk resident Colgate Darden, a former governor and former president of the University of Virginia, for a medical school in Norfolk. It was a losing battle because Colgate Darden's experience at the University of Virginia was summed up virtually as follows: "a medical school is a money-loser, and the people in charge are arrogant." It was "no sale" to one of Norfolk's most influential citizens.

The concern of some local practitioners that their hospital privileges would be compromised had generally quieted. It was not the goal of NAMCA to construct a medical school hospital. A sufficient number of teaching beds for a medical school could be found by tallying all hospital facilities across the area, including government hospitals. Agreement was reached with Norfolk General Hospital and other area hospitals, particularly with Children's Hospital of The King's Daughters and DePaul Hospital, to allow teaching.

Participation of all area hospitals on both sides of Hampton Roads fostered a feeling of inclusiveness which offset earlier resentment that some in Norfolk were presuming to plan for the Peninsula medical establishments. Furthering the commitment to make the school regional, the name NAMCA (Norfolk Area Medical Center Authority) was later changed to EVMA (Eastern Virginia Medical Authority), in 1975.

As recruitment of early faculty began, an excellent group of basic scientists came on board as the first full-time faculty. It was anticipated that local practitioners with appropriate credentials would be recruited as volunteer faculty to hasten the accreditation process.

Bob Payne, M.D., chairman of NAMCA's medical advisory committee, was deeply involved in planning and recommending programs to be incorporated into the proposed medical school's master plan.

NAMCA had appointed a special committee to research and advise on the need for a cardio-pulmonary laboratory. Harry Mansbach was among those who were instrumental in persuading the Tidewater Heart Association to contribute heavily to establishing and equipping such a laboratory at Children's Hospital of The King's Daughters.

The medical advisory committee also recommended that NAMCA move to establish a cardiac surgery department at Norfolk General Hospital. It was seen as a way to strengthen medical services in the area and as an asset in gaining accreditation as a medical school.

A. A. Douglas Moore, M.D. came to direct a cardio-pulmonary laboratory at Norfolk General Hospital in 1967 and became the very first EVMS full-time faculty member.

Dr. Norman Thomson brought his nine-member heart surgery team from Buffalo, New York, also in 1967, to start the cardiac surgery program, the only one in Virginia beyond those at the two state-supported medical schools. The groundbreaking nature of heart surgery was underscored by Norman when he recalled hearing his professor of surgery state that the heart was one organ that the surgeon's knife would never invade.

As the field represented a medical frontier, two key players, Wendall Winn and Warren White, along with Roy Prangley, administrator of Norfolk General Hospital, had required some persuading to believe in the need to establish support for a cardiac surgery program at Norfolk General Hospital prior to recruitment efforts. As it turned out, both Wendall Winn and Warren White later were open-heart surgery patients at Norfolk General Hospital.

Dr. Bruce Innes was recruited, also in 1967, to direct the cardiopulmonary research laboratory, which was also open to other legitimate researchers.

Bruce experienced an unusual introduction to his role in Norfolk. Mason met his plane on a hot summer afternoon. En route to see his official base of operation, they stopped first at a drugstore to purchase IV equipment. The second stop was the Andrews home, where Bruce was ushered into the presence of family members attending a desperately sick young dog. Evidence of a *streptococcus* infection was abundant. The memory is vivid of Bruce Innes in his crisp cord suit kneeling beside his "first patient" and skillfully inserting the IV needle into the vein of the little dog, enabling her to turn the corner toward recovery with further help from her Norfolk vet.

Doctors Moore, Thomson and Innes were attracted from excellent programs elsewhere to the programs being started by NAMCA not just to continue doing the same things, but to become involved in the teaching and research opportunities offered by the founding of a new medical school. This was a key factor many more times as the medical school moved from a plan to be marketed to a marketable attraction.

18

To School for the School

By law, appointees to NAMCA were to serve terms of no more than six consecutive years. Mason had been appointed to a three-year term by Norfolk City Council in April 1964, when NAMCA was authorized, and became NAMCA's first elected chairman at the authority's first meeting. He had been re-appointed to a second three-year term and served again as chairman, for a total of six consecutive years. Bill Woodley and John Franklin also served for six consecutive years as NAMCA commissioners.

Because members of the authority were appointed for one-, two- or three-year terms, and because eventually seven Hampton Roads political jurisdictions became appointing agents, the board of commissioners of NAMCA experienced some turnover. Through it all, the outstanding work of NAMCA's excellent advisory committees was a key to progress and continuity. But one person's leadership remained constant for these six formative years, always dreaming "the impossible dream" and demanding the pursuit of excellence of himself and others.

NAMCA elected Harry Mansbach as its second chairman in 1970 to succeed Mason. Harry had been a diligent and effective member of the NAMCA team, especially in the area of fundraising. Much remained to be done before all the conditions imposed by the AMA and AAMC for accreditation of the Eastern Virginia Medical School could be satisfied, but under Harry Mansbach and others, and with the assembling academic team, EVMS received accreditation in 1973 and admitted its first class of twenty-four students in the fall of that year. Events came full circle, as the final official accreditation team included both Vernon Wilson and Nathan Stark, President of the Kansas City Medical Center, who had given the charge to NAMCA's lay advisory committee in 1964.

NAMCA appointed Mason a consultant in order to retain his expertise and familiarity with the issues going forward. However, Mason wanted to give Harry some breathing space. He also thought it appealing to revisit the world of academic medicine as a participant. He wanted to study in the fields of endocrinology and infertility and he wanted to learn the latest educational techniques. And, of course, he wanted to be able to bring what he learned back to the long-sought EVMS. He requested and was granted a one-year lectureship at Johns Hopkins by Dr. Howard W. Jones, Jr., then acting chairman of the Department of Gynecology and Obstetrics, where Mason had completed his five-year residency twenty years earlier. His assignment was to teach Johns Hopkins students and to study in the special areas described above.

However laudable the plan, there were just one or two fine points not taken adequately into consideration by the master planner. First, there was some miscalculation on the degree of enthusiasm with which other members of the Andrews family regarded the details involving themselves. It seemed perfectly reasonable to Mason that someone, not he, would find a suitable school for their rising high school senior, who might have been anticipating graduating with her senior class in Norfolk, and would contract for an apartment, together with basic rented furniture in Baltimore. His plan also foresaw that the keys to the Norfolk house would be turned over to incoming EVMS dean Robert Manning and his family for the duration.

And so it came to pass that our daughter, fitting in by day as best she could in a close-knit class at Baltimore Friends, would join me every afternoon on the rented furniture for tea, conversation and *Star Trek* reruns. The dog, however, was pleased with her new domicile; she seemed to enjoy her newly-invented game of dropping her ball from the eighth floor balcony and watching her people retrieve it. For the retrievers, accommodating such large expectations seemed somehow emblematic of the whole adventure.

Of course, it was very good to be reunited with special friends — with Drs. Howard and Georgeanna Seegar Jones at Johns Hopkins — and with others known over the ten years in which Mason had trained there (four years medical school and five years residency, with wartime Navy experience wedged in between). They, as well as new colleagues, all contributed to the remarkable and enviable intellectual atmosphere where expert consultation was available on the spot, in the doctors' dining room, or traversing the corridors. There was an almost palpable energy everywhere. Dr. Georgeanna Jones was extremely generous in bringing Mason abreast of the latest progress and challenges in reproductive medicine.

The Jones's hospitality extended to pleasant sailing on their boat, *Aphrodite*, trailing her dinghy, *Hermaphrodite* (the latter alluding to some groundbreaking medical work in which the Joneses were involved). Conversation on board took on a distinctly scientific tone.

19

Continuing to Lead

It seems interesting in retrospect to trace the ties from the seemingly free-standing Baltimore experiences to other Andrews projects and "impossible dreams." After the family returned to Norfolk from Baltimore, Mason was appointed Founding Chairman of Obstetrics and Gynecology at the newly accredited Eastern Virginia Medical School. The need to recruit faculty and residents and fellows for his department now faced this man who sometimes referred to himself as an academic retread, but who knew how to shoot for the moon.

Perhaps the eleven-day Gibson Island sailboat cruise we had taken with the Drs. Jones while we were living in Baltimore had provided Mason a pivotal opportunity with a captive audience to promote EVMS. As it turned out, when Howard and Georgeanna reached mandatory retirement age at Hopkins they allowed themselves to be recruited to Norfolk and to the Department of Obstetrics and Gynecology at EVMS. In a very brief time they had brought international acclaim to the fledgling medical school with their historically successful in vitro fertilization program. Rumor had it then that Hopkins authorities were left wondering why they had not devised an exception to their mandatory retirement age policy.

And again, perhaps it was not surprising to discover that Mason, the amateur city planner, still had the unrealized potential of "this old seaport city," Norfolk, in his sights. This long-standing vision had once included private citizen Mason Andrews seeking out advice on urban renewal (James W. Rouse's neologism) from Jim Rouse in 1956. That long-standing relationship was strengthened during this time in Baltimore.

It was very good to continue friendship on a closer basis with Jim and Libby Rouse. Their hospitality included making their Columbia, Maryland, house on Windstream Drive available to the Andrews family at the conclusion of the Friends School term. It was an inspiration to

Georgeanna Seegar Jones, M.D. and Howard W. Jones, Jr., M.D.

experience in their company their dream of an ideal community becoming a reality as Columbia unfolded. As things worked out in this time frame, Mason was taking night call for the Hopkins alliance with Columbia's health system, and in this capacity he delivered Jim and Libby's grandson "Jimbo."

Jim became essential to the revitalization of downtown Norfolk when Mason trained his sights on this target, by his decision and his underwriting of Waterside, which is considered the key that allowed downtown Norfolk to begin its transformation.

Mason never retired because there was always more that he wanted to do. In addition to enjoying his patients, his students, and his professional career, his activities would come to include twenty-six years on Norfolk City Council as councilman, vice-mayor and mayor and as chairman of the Mayor's Advisory Committee to address ambitious city renewal — the project he loved best. His family members hope that Mason, while busily considering his list of things to do, allowed himself to savor for a moment the graduation of the first class of students at Eastern Virginia Medical School.

AFTERWORD

DATA ARE AVAILABLE in the Old Dominion University library archives relative to Mason Andrews' professional and civic careers. Documentation of matters addressed in these chapters, delivered into the keeping of an early EVMS librarian, have been lost. Some documentation has been recoverable in personal files and through the assistance of some who were closely involved in these matters. The valuable contributions of many additional participants, rendered anonymous by this loss, are gratefully acknowledged. This history is based primarily on newspaper accounts and on personal experience of Andrews family members and of other involved persons who have read the text for accuracy. Documentation dating from the appointment of the first dean, Robert T. Manning, M.D., and early full-time faculty is, presumably, available in the EVMS archives.

RESOLUTIONS OF APPRECIATION

ADOPTED MAY 11, 1970:

WHEREAS, Mason C. Andrews, M.D., has served the Norfolk Area Medical Center Authority with complete and absolute devotion from the time it was created by an Act of the Virginia General Assembly on April 28, 1964, first as a Commissioner and since June 2, 1964 as its Chairman, and

WHEREAS, Mason Andrews has provided the highest and finest example of public service by his inspired guidance, unstinting efforts and total commitment to the development of a relatively small medical core into the presently vibrant and excellent Medical Center, which clearly prophesies the imminent creation of the Eastern Virginia Medical School, and

· WHEREAS, the law creating the Authority does not permit Mason Andrews to be reappointed a Commissioner, having served the legal maximum of two full terms, each for three years,

NOW, THEREFORE, BE IT RESOLVED that the Norfolk Area Medical Center Authority accepts the legally dictated resignation of Dr. Andrews with deep regret, and with great appreciation notes that his enormous mental and physical energy and efforts, and his development of support and favorable opinion within the legal, legislative, cultural, medical, business and professional communications, are largely responsible for the astonishing growth of the Medical Center and the fruition of the plans for creating the Eastern Virginia Medical School, Dr. Andrews having created the climate under which these plans have achieved such remarkable success and made such amazing progress; and

BE IT FURTHER RESOLVED that the Authority cites Dr. Andrews, who will always be known affectionately as "Chairman Andrews" to the other Commissioners, for his clear vision, steadfastness of spirit, unswerving devotion and absolute dedication to the completion of the difficult task of establishing a Medical School of excellence in eastern Virginia and for his humble belief in the proposition that man's best effort is made on behalf of his fellow man; and

BE IT FURTHER RESOLVED that the Norfolk Area Medical Center Authority takes comfort in the knowledge that Dr. Andrews has agreed to serve as Chairman of the Eastern Virginia Medical School Planning and Development Committee, where his unique talents will continue to benefit our entire area and assures the realization of his ultimate goal — THE EASTERN VIRGINIA MEDICAL SCHOOL.

Harry H. Marshall
Chairman

Lawrence V. Breeff
Attest

APPENDIX 1
Resolution by Norfolk Area Medical Center Authority

ndiford Motor Hotel
DITIONED UNITS — SWIMMING POOL — TELEPHONES
FREE TELEVISION IN EVERY ROOM
RESTAURANT & COCKTAIL LOUNGE — ROOM SERVICE
WATTERSON EXPRESSWAY & FREEDOM WAY AT STANDIFORD AIRPORT
LOUISVILLE, KENTUCKY 40221
AREA CODE 502 PHONE: 366-4511

Executive Offices:
Suite 811
3300 West Mockingbird Lane
Dallas, Texas 75235
Phone: 357-5601
Area Code: 214

April 19, 1970

Dear Mason,

This is the first chance I have had to do a little catching up on letters and other items. For several weeks I have had the enclosed two color slides and prints for you and Dr. Ruffin. I hope they remind each of you of a productive meeting.

The development of new medical centers, as well as maintaining existing ones, certainly calls for unusual fortitude and conviction these days. I have just returned from giving a seminar at the University of Kentucky in Lexington where I found my old friends and home plagued by limited state revenue and university appropriations.

We are in a paradoxical position. Relations, understanding, cooperative interests, and general support is excellent with our university, professional, and civic colleagues. The National

APPENDIX 2
Letter from Richardson K. Noback, M.D., of April 19, 1970

Advisory Council has recommended funding the school in the amount we requested and the hospital at 80% of our application. Architects are poised. Of course, we must have state committment to construction and operation yet the voters defeated the increased tax rate which would have handled schools and our program. Now we wait on a 60 day legislature session which started on the 15th. Much work, of course, to help people reach the hoped for answer. In fact, we are looking at some local fund raising as a back-up possibility; in this case rather following in your footsteps!

    I hope your efforts and leadership are bringing the Tidewater area and NAMCA ever closer to such important objectives. At times words are difficult and seem clumsey. I am aware of some changes later this month. I simply want to express my great appreciation and admiration for the consistency, quality, and vision of your leadership in the affairs of NAMCA. While the road is long, you must have substantial satisfaction in the many important roles you are filling.

    Nan joins me in sending you, Sabina, and the girls our very best wishes.

                              Dick

THE UNIVERSITY OF KANSAS
RAINBOW BOULEVARD AT 39TH
AREA CODE 913

MEDICAL CENTER
KANSAS CITY, KANSAS 66103
TELEPHONE 236-5252

OFFICE OF THE VICE-CHANCELLOR
FOR HEALTH AFFAIRS

20 May 1971

Dear Mason,

I send you this letter at home as I wish it to convey to you some personal thoughts that are beyond any official relationship that exists between us.

It has been clear to me since our first meeting that you are now and will continue to be the spiritual strength of the past, present and future of the Medical School. I welcome your strength and guidance as I make my contribution to the idea that you so clearly generated, nourished and sustained. I have come to a beginning realization of the magnitude of your effort and sacrifice in the past few weeks and your discussion at the meeting of the Planning and Development Committee with the site team provided additional evidence in support of my intuition about your personal philosophy. Too often I see men simply believe that which they do and have done throughout their lives. You are

APPENDIX 3
Letter from Robert T. Manning, M.D., of May 20, 1971

THE UNIVERSITY OF KANSAS MEDICAL CENTER

RAINBOW BOULEVARD AT 39TH
AREA CODE 913

KANSAS CITY, KANSAS 66103
TELEPHONE 236-5252

OFFICE OF THE VICE-CHANCELLOR
FOR HEALTH AFFAIRS

among that rare cadre of men who do what they believe. Men who perceive a need, establish therefrom a goal and commit themselves to its attainment.

We now have reached the end of the beginning on the path to fulfilling the School's reality. What talents I have to offer are completely committed to their fulfillment in the most creative way that I can marshall them. I have no broader ambitions than to be, as you say, "my own best self." I hope that self is sufficient to the task ahead. Your wisdom and sustaining strength will continue to be needed by us all and particularly by me.

I look forward to many moments of reflection with you now that immediate hectic deadlines are for the time behind us. I apologize for not having created such opportunity.

The future has always looked bright to me — a heritage from my mother and father. The bright future now before us seems beyond my wildest anticipation and I am eternally grateful to you for allowing me, however sureptitiously, to share your dream and to help, however my efforts afford to help carry it into reality. With affectionate respect

University of Missouri – Columbia

M-402 Medical Sciences
Columbia, Mo. 65201

SCHOOL OF MEDICINE
Department of Community Health and Family Medicine

Telephone
314-882-8781

March 2, 1973

Mason C. Andrews, M.D.
Chairman
Department of Obstetrics
   and Gynecology
Eastern Virginia Medical School
901 & 903 Medical Tower
Norfolk, Virginia 23507

Dear Mason:

It was good to hear from you. Sam Black also brought greetings from you yesterday at the Rotary Club. Both Nathan and I were somewhat apprehensive about the role in which we found ourselves while trying to be of further service to the School at Norfolk but hope that the contribution did move you one step closer to the quality of performance which everyone desires without having introduced any needless obstructions.

The issue of "faint praise" was fairly well cleared up in our minds by the time we had finished the survey but somewhat after you had visited with us. I have some feeling that the membership of the Foundation has more insight into it than perhaps the Commissioners. In any event I could not agree more that you are one of the strong leaders within the community and without your efforts the School neither would have gotten as far as it has nor as a matter of fact would have much of a chance in the future since it is because of our faith in you and your own judgment that people like Nathan and myself continue to be involved.

It will not take a great deal of adaptation as you indicate in order to bring the Medical School through its next phase of development. It is going to require a sensitivity and sharpness of judgment which has not as yet been strongly in evidence in

APPENDIX 4
Letter from Vernon E. Wilson, M.D., March 2, 1973

Mason C. Andrews
March 2, 1973
page two

the Administration of the School and places a tremendous burden upon Dick McGraw. Whether Dick's immediate past experience has given him this kind of expertise can only be judged from his performance. Certainly his early decisions will be crucial ones.

My own role in trying to be of help is of course a very complicated one. The fact that I have been absent from the scene as a direct advisor now qualifies me to work on your behalf at the level of the Council on Medical Education to be sure that they do have a full understanding of the issues and review the project in an objective manner. If I become personally involved in consulting with EVMS it would be necessary for me to again disqualify myself in the national role. Perhaps you may want to give some thought to renewing your exchanges with Dick Noback who has the same kinds of insight although he may not at times be quite so abrupt in stating them.

In any event your kind invitation to come for a personal visit will be carefully kept in the uppermost part of our agenda should we come East anytime in the near future. That could possibly be this summer at the time of the AMA meetings.

Best personal regards,

Vernon E. Wilson, M.D.
Professor of Community Health
and Medical Practice

VEW:kc

University of Missouri – Columbia

M-402 Medical Sciences
Columbia, Mo. 65201

SCHOOL OF MEDICINE
Department of Community Health and Family Medicine

Telephone
314-882-3940

June 15, 1973

Mason C. Andrews, M.D.
901 & 903 Medical Tower
Norfolk, Virginia 23507

Dear Mason:

    It was good to hear from you in your note of June 7 and you need not appologize for the rapid passage of time. It must be a characteristic of people who have too many things going at the same time since it only seems like yesterday that I was in Norfolk with you.

    Hopefully the shakedown process for the Medical School will continue to edge toward the original aspirations we all had for it, although the process is never as easy or as simple as it seems it will be upon initiation. We didn't have much of a chance to discuss the administrative issues which lay behind the final resolution of your search for leadership and that might well provide us with an interesting opportunity to visit when we do get together. The selection of leadership is always the end result of a series of compromises and it does little good to look backward and speculate on how things might have been different.

    Our own plans for coming to the East coast have been altered a bit both because of the tentative change in the obligations I will have in New York City and the fact that I now have a workshop on Technology in Health Care in New Hampshire in August. If the gasoline shortage permits us in all probability will be coming through about the middle of August. Once we get a little closer to the date and if it looks as though we will be able to make the trip, I will be back in touch with you with more specific dates and times to be sure that we'll be convenient for you and Sabine.

    It was good to hear from you and I hope we can stay in touch.

Best personal regards,

Vernon E. Wilson
Professor of Community Health
    and Medical Practice

VEW/bnp

APPENDIX 5
Letter from Vernon E. Wilson, M.D. of June 15, 1973

EASTERN VIRGINIA MEDICAL SCHOOL
DEPARTMENT OF INTERNAL MEDICINE
600 GRESHAM DRIVE
NORFOLK, VIRGINIA 23507

TELEPHONE (804) 441-3584

Dec 6, 1976

ROBERT T. MANNING, M.D.
Professor and Chairman

PERSONAL

December 6, 1976

Mason Andrews, M.D.
Professor and Chairman
Department of Obstetrics
 & Gynecology
600 Gresham Drive
Norfolk, Virginia 23507

Dear Mason:

    The decision to return to Kansas was much more difficult to make than the one six years ago to join in the development of the Eastern Virginia Medical School. Whatever success may have marked my efforts here, I have always been acutely aware that they were built on a solid foundation that you more than anyone else established in the professional and lay community. My debt to you for the opportunity to participate in this venture is unrepayable.

    My personal regard for you both as a person and physician is without equal. Your contributions to the community and School continue to be inadequately recognized, in my opinion, but I want you to know I personally regard you as a first citizen and first physician. If at any time I can be of service to you or your family personally or professionally, I would be honored to respond to your wishes.

    With warm personal regards, I remain,

                              Sincerely,

                              Robert T. Manning, M.D.
                            Professor and Chairman
                            Department of Medicine

RTM/pbs

APPENDIX 6

Letter from Robert T. Manning, M.D. of December 6, 1976

Richardson K. Noback, M.D.
2912 Abercorn Drive
Las Vegas, Nevada 89134

23 July 2008

When the individuals in a community are making substantial improvements, it is evident that many have worked effectively to set the stage for changes. The NAMCA pioneers were one of those remarkable groups who proved sufficiently able, sufficiently dedicated, sufficiently trustworthy, and sufficiently generous of their resources, time and talent to bring to life a truly noble effort to benefit legions of individuals in their then present as well as in the more distant future.

All those who play roles in social engineering necessary to significant changes in a society learn the value of generalizations several of which follow. There are many who are able to analyze, plan, research, study, and write about problems. These are appropriate activities but they have no operational impact unless they lead to action. Leadership is the name we give to the ability to bring together the concepts, individuals, purposes, and resources necessary to respond to problems in our society.

Enlightened leadership calls for many characteristics and capacities. Earned respect for competence in a valued occupation is one. Vision of a better way of dealing with problems is another. Personal standards and integrity are necessary to earn trust. High intelligence coupled to imagination is needed. Determination, high energy levels, and stamina are vital as is an earned measure of self-confidence. The ability to focus, to transmit enthusiasm, to encourage, to be optimistic and resilient, and to place the shared accomplishments of the group ahead of personal role are major assets. Strength of character and of conviction, courtesy and kindness are valuable assets. Knowledge of history in general and of the specific problems is required to understand the big picture and so be a statesman rather than a successful technician. The ability to communicate effectively is vital just as listening is as important as talking or writing.

Realism makes clear that those who combine such characteristics are rare. There is a wise observation that anyone is fortunate who meets a handful of such individuals in a lifetime.

The Commonwealth and the Tidewater had such an individual in the development of EVMS. He served as the Chairman of the Norfolk Area Medical Center Authority. In addition to this and other large roles Dr. Mason Andrews served as Mayor of Norfolk. Those of us who have served both as busy clinicians and in community roles know how much is demanded of anyone who earns the respect and trust of professional colleagues and then of citizens active in community affairs. To carry so many roles for so many years and with great distinction requires the highest abilities and personal characteristics.

APPENDIX 7

Commentary by Richardson K. Noback, of July 23, 2008

Perhaps it is appropriate to comment on some personal observations. Dr. Andrews was a tall, powerful, graceful man with a courteous manner. He was a gracious host, a devoted husband and father, an easy conversationalist who had little time for small talk, and a keen observer. His conversation was precise yet always respectful. One recognized quickly that he possessed a remarkable intellect which he kept under gentle control to accomplish the best and the most in every circumstance. His range of information was extensive which reflected his range of interests.

I can recall no instances when such an array of capabilities was directed to any purpose other than to ring out the best in a setting. Superficial cleverness was not an interest. Dr. Andrews had what Alfred North Whitehead called style – the disciplined use of power – along with the ability to deliver what appears to be effortless excellence which those who share his characteristic know comes from much hard work.

For years I have used his example one noon to stimulate others to high standards of performance. I was in Norfolk on one of my visits as the Executive Medical Consultant to NAMCA. At noon the Mayor was to preside over a major luncheon in the main ballroom to recognize those who had made notable contributions to the City in the preceding year. After the meal, Dr. Andrews rose to speak. With no notes he proceeded to recognize each person in the ballroom by name and role along with a few additional comments. He did this easily, gracefully, and without a single stumble.

Richardson K. Noback, M.D.
2912 Abercorn Drive
Las Vegas, Nevada 89134

You invited comments on <u>From Where I Stood: The Birth Of A Medical School</u>. I consider it a special privilege to offer the following paragraphs. But first I would like to set some context for what follows.

Over many years I have had the duty to read a great deal, write frequently, and edit or modify the prose efforts of others. This experience sharpens one's perceptions while it tends to make one quick to pick up a pencil for questions or suggestions for changes in a written piece. It also teaches that excellent writing is difficult work. When the words sing, you know that someone with special talents has worked both hard and competently to construct the piece.

As I began this assignment, the force of habit had me pencil in notes such as the active voice as much more powerful than the passive voice and a few other standard or mechanical comments. Soon I put down my pencil except for a very few suggestions which deal with facts or questions of clarification where I believe a word or two may have been omitted. These are only minor technical details. Some other much more important elements shine from the pages.

The author has a distinct, authentic voice. This is consistent through the narrative. The voice is that of an observant, secure, perceptive, gentle yet strong lady who is at home in a variety of settings. She has a wide background of experiences in the many activities required for the social

APPENDIX 8
Editorial perspective, Richardson K. Noback, M.D., of September 17, 2008

engineering which is an integral part of any large community project. The voice reveals an optimistic, loyal, competent lady of great capacity and of good humor.

While styles of writing vary and some editors tend to guide or force prose into the styles they judge best, I would not change anything more that a word or two here and there for the reasons previously noted. The author's words do sing as she tells her story. Her style is consistent. Some of her phrasing is gifted. The vignettes of home life make the man and the story real as well as compelling. This is no artificial piece constructed for someone by a hired hand. It engages one's attention and holds it. The narrative will be real years from now.

There is an important element in the work. This may not be apparent unless one has lived through the birth and early development of academic medical centers. Such developments are complex since medicine itself extends into so many sectors of current society. In some accounts of such enterprises authors dwell on intricate details, clashes between power blocks, personalities, or excessive attention to individuals and groups.

Mrs. Andrews chooses carefully to guide the reader to consider major principles, major developments, and major players in the drama. She includes enough detail to make plain just how much the visionaries accomplished. She stresses the goals and values basic to real progress in a free society.

There is one paragraph which belongs in a position of prominence in any academic setting. It is particularly appropriate for every academic medical center.

"Over the course of many years of his civic activities the notion of teamwork was refined into what he called The Process. The Process consisted of assembling "everyone around the same table at the same time." "Everyone" meant board, staff, the best possible consultants, and others as appropriate for "everyone to be on the same page" at all times. He believed that The Process was, in fact, the easiest and most direct path to the desired result and that it tended to eliminate costly problems "down the road." It seemed so simple to follow The Process – It simply required integrity of motivation and respect for the advice of the best other voices. He argued that it led consistently to achievement."

In short, Mrs. Andrews spins together principles, specifics, and narrative to fashion a rope which holds the reader's attention securely as she tells a compelling story.

                                    RKN   Las Vegas   17 September 2008

CHRONOLOGY OF EVMS DEVELOPMENT (draft)

1959   Lawrence Cox proposed medical school and talked to Ryan Club.

1960   At dedication of Medical Tower, Cox further proposes medical school.

1960   At invitation of Drs. Charles Horton and Mason Andrews, Dr. Vernon Wilson, Dean of University of Missouri Medical School, first visits Norfolk and begins 10 years as gratuitous advisor to the medical school effort.

1961   President of Norfolk Academy of Medicine (Mason Andrews) appoints committee to study medical school proposal. Dr. Glen Leymaster from the AMA and Dr. Lee Powers from the Association of American Medical Colleges visit Norfolk at invitation of Medical Society and conclude that the clinical facilities and population size are appropriate bases for a new medical school. They suggest coordination with the State educational system.

1961   Norfolk Academy of Medicine endorses establishment of medical school.

1962   Delegate Warren White pursuing the request of the Medical Society introduces successful legislation requiring a study of medical education in Virginia and Hampton Roads by the State Council of Higher Education.

Statewide Advisory Committee headed by Mr. Tom Boushall established for this purpose. Mason Andrews, Hampton Roads representative.

1962   Mayor Roy Martin of Norfolk appoints the Mayors Advisory Committee on the establishment of a medical school in Norfolk. Mr. Barron Black, Chairman. The Brief prepared for this committee at Mr. Black's request by M. Andrews and submitted to the State Council of High Education Committee.

1963   State Council of Higher Education Advisory Committee after 18 months of exploration and meetings (including interviews with Drs. Leymaster and Powers) recommends establishment of the third school, in Hampton Roads, privately financed.

1963   Working with Planning Council of the United Communities. M. Andrews and George Rice assemble group of interested citizens to explore development of medical school and medical center. Group includes Toy Savage, Bob Payne, John Franklin, Larry Cox, Dick Welton and Harry Price. Continues consultation with Vern Wilson and persons nationally respected in medical center planning and medical school operation (here and in Washington). It writes specific legislative proposal for the establishment of an authority.

APPENDIX 9
Mason C. Andrews' 1983 Draft Timeline

1964 Report of State Council of Higher Education approves report concerning a medical school in Hampton Roads. State legislature adopts legislation establishing an Authority for the purpose of establishing and operating a medical school and planning a medical center. It granted this Authority power of eminent domain and the power to borrow money. Seven Authority members appointed by Norfolk City Council including M. Andrews, Chairman, Toy Savage, Larry Cox, John Franklin, Walter Page, ~~and Lee Payne~~.

Vincent Kling employed as architect to plan medical center. Dr. Richardson Noback, Dean, University of Missouri Medical School at Kansas City, engaged as a medical school program planner - supervised by Vernon Wilson. Precise planning document including goals and steps toward achieving a medical center and medical school prepared by Noback and adopted by Authority. Physical plans including expansion of a medical center, east and south, designed by Kling. Medical Advisory Committee headed by Dr. Robert Payne began regular productive meetings. Lay Advisory Committee formed including most of the recognized civic leaders. Initial meeting addressed by Nathan Stark, President of Kansas City Medical Center and Executive Vice President of Hallmark Cards emphasized the importance of teaching and research to the quality of medical care in an environment.

1966 Physical plan for site expansion approved by City Council.

1967 Invasive Heart Laboratory established. Dr. Douglas Moore recruited.

1968 Heart surgery program moved en mass from Buffalo. Eleven persons headed by Norman Thompson.

1969 Rehabilitation Institute built by Authority. Planning for mental health institute begun.

1969 Dr. James Etheridge recruited as faculty member in pediatric neurology.

~~1969~~ Conference of Medical Educators held at Virginia Beach including Deans and college Presidents from Virginia medical schools, Tufts, University of Missouri, Vermont, and the Director of the National Institutes of Health. Plans for a medical school in Hampton Roads were reexamined and the direction reaffirmed.

1970 City of Norfolk agrees to provide $500,000 annually for the operation of the school. Campaign Committee formed headed by Porter Hardy. Brochure prepared for $15 million campaign.

1971 Legislation authorizes study of proposed medical school as a potential recipient of a per student subsidy.

1972 Per student subsidy approved by legislature.

1973 Accreditation of the school by the Association of American Medical Colleges. Dr. Vernon Wilson was Chairman of the Committee investigating the school. Another member of the Committee was Nathan Stark.

1974 M. Andrews appointed Chairman of Obstetrics and Gynecology. Built accredited residency program from 12 to 20. Academic department grew to include subspecialties of maternal and fetal medicine, oncology, and reproductive medicine. It included genetics and general obstetrics and gynecology.

1978 Drs. Howard and Georgeanna Jones joined the department and proceeded to develop a program in reproductive medicine which is recognized for excellence nationally and internationally.

1983 Jones Institute founded and Dr. Gary Hodgen recruited from National Institutes of Health to add world class basic science to the reproductive medicine division of the department.

NOTE: Dates are from recollection and may well vary by a year or so.

EVMS to name building for Mason Andrews

January 25, 2007

NORFOLK—EVMS will rename one of its most prominent buildings in memory of Dr. Mason C. Andrews, a medical pioneer and prime mover behind the medical school's creation.

EVMS President Harry T. Lester made the announcement during a ceremony Thursday in McCombs Auditorium where doctors, faculty members, students, staff and civic leaders paid tribute to the doctor, teacher and medical school founder whose efforts not only gave birth to EVMS, but also reshaped much of Norfolk.

Andrews made international headlines in December 1981 when he delivered the first baby conceived by in-vitro fertilization.

Andrews Hall
Eastern Virginia Medical School

Architect's rendering of Mason C. Andrews Hall
High-resolution image (2.3 megabytes)

"Dr. Andrews touched the lives of many individuals and many organizations," said Lester. "But I think it is fair to say that EVMS held a special place in his heart. I know he held a special one in ours."

Andrews, who passed away in the fall of 2006 at the age of 87, was a pioneering obstetrician who pushed EVMS to the forefront of reproductive medicine.

Andrews "was a giant in medicine," said Dean and Provost Gerald J. Pepe, Ph.D. "Not only nationally but internationally."

Andrews' longtime friend and colleague Howard W. Jones, M.D., a professor emeritus of obstetrics and gynecology and co-founder of the EVMS Jones Institute for Reproductive Medicine, reflected on Andrews' relentless drive and his passion for excellence and community service.

EVMS President Harry Lester presents a framed copy of the program and sketch of Andrews Hall to Sabine Andrews and her family.

Jones compared Andrews to Izaak Walton, whose "Compleat Angler" recounted the way he applied science to the art of fishing three centuries ago.

"Mason was a complete physician," said Jones. "And he expected everyone else to be complete physicians as well."

Born in Norfolk, Va., Andrews earned his undergraduate degree from Princeton University in 1940 and his medical degree from the Johns Hopkins School of Medicine. After completing a tour in the U.S. Navy and finishing his residency at Johns Hopkins in the early 1950s, he returned to Norfolk and began talking about the need to create a medical school in the region.

Andrews and a group of visionary community leaders worked tirelessly to lobby for official sanction and raised $17 million required to establish the medical school. In 1973, EVMS opened its doors.

APPENDIX 10
EVMS announcement concerning Andrews Hall, 2007

"Mason taught me the importance of giving back to your community and medical specialty by the example he set as he worked to convince the community of the importance of establishing a medical school in Hampton Roads," LeHew said. "He spent countless hours in planning sessions, meetings and discussions with community and state leaders cause he was determined to get the job done. He never wavered from his vision."

As first chairman of the EVMS Department of Obstetrics and Gynecology, Andrews propelled the young medical school to the forefront in reproductive medicine when he recruited Jones and his late wife, Georgeanna S. Jones, M.D., from Johns Hopkins.

The trio launched groundbreaking research resulted in the Dec. 28, 1981, birth of Elizabeth Jordan Carr, the nation's first child conceived through in-vitro fertilization. Andrews delivered Carr. Continuing success in in-vitro fertilization led to the creation in 1983 of the Jones Institute for Reproductive Medicine.

Alfred Abuhamad, M.D., chairman of the Department of Obstetrics and Gynecology, noted that Andrews' cutting-edge research spanned six decades, beginning with a study published in 1940 when Andrews was just 21 and continuing until not long before his death at age 87.

"His clear vision, his tenacity and persistence on doing the right thing has laid the foundation for a great medical school and an ob-gyn department that achieved national and international distinction," said Abuhamad.

Andrews also had an enormous impact on the rest of the community. Elected to the City Council in Norfolk 1974, he served as mayor from 1992 to 1994 and his efforts at urban renewal helped spark the revival that has transformed Norfolk.

Fairfax Hall, which will soon be renovated, will become Andrews Hall after completion in December 2008. The naming of the building and the creation the Mason C. Andrews Citizen-Scholar Award are meant as enduring testaments to Andrews' accomplishments.

Abuhamad noted Andrews' key role in transforming a relative medical backwater into the vibrant hub of medical institutions that draws patients from surrounding states.

"Two-thousand, six hundred medical student graduates, 152 fully trained obstetrics and gynecology residents of whom, 54 are still practicing in Hampton Roads today," Abuhamad said. "The legacy and the vision of Dr. Mason Andrews live on."

www.ingramcontent.com/pod-product-compliance
Lightning Source LLC
Chambersburg PA
CBHW071739090426
42738CB00011B/2532